Everywoman's Guide To Travel

Everywoman's Guide To Travel

Donna Goldfein

LES FEMMES PUBLISHING
Millbrae, California

I dedicate this book to my many friends with American Airlines who share my love of people and travel.

Cover Design and Illustration by Brent Beck
Interior Illustrations by Gilbert Goldfein

Copyright © 1977 by Donna Goldfein

Published by LES FEMMES
231 Adrian Road
Millbrae, California 94030

First printing, October 1977
Made in the United States of America

Library of Congress Cataloging in Publication Data

Goldfein, Donna, 1933-
  Everywoman's guide to travel.

  Bibliography: p.
  Includes index.
  1. Travel.   I. Title.
G151.G64   910'.2'4042   77-79883
ISBN 0-89087-930-3

1   2   3   4   5   6   7 — 82   81   80   79   78   77

CONTENTS

...fly the ocean in a silver plane

That simple line changed the course of my life. Funny how the words of a song can click at the exact moment your energies are ready to be channeled to a new and clear direction.

Has that happened to you? Ever? Have you ever heard a few words of a song or speech and WOW!! That's it! That is where you want to be.

The car radio blared Jo Stafford's voice over the small midwest station as I was racing the speed limit somewhere near the Iowa border, headed toward Albert Lea, Minnesota. Fresh out of college, the long summer seemed to stretch forever. My original enthusiasm for teaching seemed to grow dimmer and I was caught with a restlessness that wouldn't go away. Suddenly the answer was clear—"fly the ocean in a silver plane . . . " I would and I did.

Air travel became part of my life, starting with a job in reservations; shifting into the excitement of flying as a career, and now, working on a part time basis for American Airlines. Memories of the hundreds of trips I flew as an airline stewardess are crystal clear in my mind and I have shared some of those highlights in this book.

When my publishers heard me constantly chattering about business trips, planning holidays and our family vacations, they encouraged me to put my suggestions, hints and experiences about travel into book form. The result is a simple, condensed, step-by-step guideline that will take the trouble out of and put the pleasure into travel. I have tried to capture the carefree and eager attitude essential to thoroughly delightful travel. Women traveling today need realistic information. For instance, an assertive vocabulary becomes necessary when the desk clerk tells you he has no record of your reservation. I will teach you what to say and, equally important, what not to say to assert your control. You will learn how to avoid—being seated at a poor table in a restaurant; feeling awkward while dining alone; being taken for an extended taxi ride in a strange city. Proven solutions are offered for dealing with difficult situations.

For every woman who wants to travel with less luggage and still have plenty to wear, turn to the "Space Saver Secret" in the chapter on packing. You'll also find these pages well seasoned with tidbits of information such as: A miniature travel iron can be found in every hotel or motel room in the form of a warmed light bulb. It can be removed and used to carefully "iron" the travel creases from lightweight clothes. A spring type clothespin will hold draperies closed to shut out the early morning sun when you want to sleep late. And because a good night's sleep is so essential to the enjoyment of travel, one of the first things I pack is a pair or two of beeswax earplugs.

Hats, wigs or turbans will hold their shape beautifully, perched atop inflated balloons taped to the top of your bureau. Use club soda as an instant spot remover. A splash of vodka makes an excellent hair rinse, and used tea bags over your eyelids while you rest provide soothing relief for tired eyes and reduce puffiness. Shampoo doubles as an instant bubble bath.

Practical hints can be surprisingly useful and help to balance the serious side of travel planning and purchasing. Travel is an investment and I have emphasized that with proper planning you should never sacrifice comfort for economy. By following the guidelines suggested in the first chapters, you will be in control of the cost and full attention can be given to the pleasure of your trip.

One of the early questions which arose when this book was being planned was whether it should be directed to the woman traveling alone or to the woman traveling under any circumstances. One asked, "Should it have a chapter on traveling with children?" To which another well-seasoned traveler, and mother, replied, "Of course! A woman is *never* more alone that when she is traveling with children!"

You will also find a chapter on International Travel. It is not intended to be all inclusive since such an attempt would be impractical for these purposes. Instead, I have tried only to kindle the fires of your imagination and urge you to discover the delights of other countries, their cultures, and their people for yourself.

I am especially grateful to De Ette Loubell for sharing her extensive library of travel books with me for use in my research. I want to express my appreciation to the travelers whom I interviewed and who gave me permission to use their comments and to the librarians who helped locate reference materials for me. Thanks also to the travel agents and editors who responded to my requests for information and whose answers and suggestions I value highly. The years of travel with my husband, Danny, and our children, Dana, David and Dean, have been the source of much of the joy of travel that I share in this writing.

My immediate advice on travel is to stop thinking and start doing. As you read on you will be caught up in my enthusiasm for and love of travel. Don't let any more time slip by—come along, I'll show you the way.

I keep six honest serving men
(They taught me all I knew.)
Their names are What and Why and When
And How and Where and Who.
                    —Rudyard Kipling

THINK ABOUT IT

Travel can be equated with freedom. It provides a release from routine, a break from boredom, and an opportunity for adventure. It can give you the marvelous feeling of leisure, the luxury of personal and private hours. Travel and freedom are perfect partners and offer an opportunity to grow in new dimensions.

But let me share Amy's past four vacation years. I select her interview from the many women with whom I spoke regarding their travel experiences. Amy confessed she was a victim of returning to the same resort each year because her roommate wanted her to come along and she didn't want to disappoint her, nor did she want to take off for a new destination alone.

Interviews with other women, in varied situations, touched the same sensitive nerve and the theme was repetitious. Sometimes a sister going with sister; a niece following as companion to her aunt—and why? An honest appraisal revealed the lack of courage or initiative to change.

Are you one of those who lives others' priorities? The

price is high! You can't measure in dollars the lost opportunities and pleasure you may be sacrificing if a vacation ends leaving you somewhat disappointed.

Judith Viorst offers a touch of wry humor to what really happens when the years slip by and you may have failed to reach out and enjoy the moment.

> *"While I was thinking I was just a girl*
> *my future turned into my past.*
> *The time for wild kisses goes fast and it's*
> *Time for Sanka.*
> *Already?"**

Think about your past trips. Have you felt obligated to use vacation time visiting relatives? Such vacations can be fine if you have young children and your parents rejoice in the opportunity to see and enjoy you and their grandchildren. However, many of the persons I interviewed spoke longingly of the day they might enjoy a holiday of their own. I borrow the term "holiday" from the British—a period of rest and/or recreation. All trips should provide relaxation and time to recharge one's physical and mental batteries. If the habit of vacationing "back home" has become a routine, it may not, in reality, be a holiday in that sense of the word. But the alternatives may generate feelings of uncertainty and fear of the unknown. These emotions are natural when one approaches something for the first time. Perhaps the perfect answer to such a dilemma is a compromise between the two. Spend half the time visiting relatives and the other half doing exactly what *you* want to do. Sound good?

Or is yours a totally different situation? Are you the one all eyes turned to when the boss said, "Let's send a woman this time"? Traveling on business is often considered an exhausting experience. It doesn't have to be. Not if you plan realistically and schedule definite time for yourself. After all, you're not expected to spend twenty-four hours a day on the

---

*How Did I Get to be 40 and Other Atrocities (New York: Simon & Schuster, Inc., 1973).

job when you are in town; why should you when you are out of town? As you cultivate a new attitude toward holiday travel, develop a new concept of business travel also. View it as a combination of productive efforts and a change of pace that offers refreshment and relaxation. You'll do an even better job and look forward to it as a real opportunity.

It is wise to take paper and pencil when you first sit down to consider a short holiday, business trip or annual vacation. Often a wonderful, spontaneous idea is lost or forgotten unless the message is delegated to paper.

Close your eyes for a moment and give full thought to any plans you may have for your next trip. Is your vacation time clearly marked on your calendar—or have you been putting off a decision this year because you aren't ready to repeat another annual vacation with a relative or roommate? Often one allows the financial savings or security of companionship in sharing a trip to rob one of the great freedom of the "solo traveler." We will deal honestly with the fears and questions you may have about traveling alone. But reading other women's testimonials will never equal experiencing the thrill and the excitement of travel freedom. George Bernard Shaw once remarked: "If you teach a man anything, he will never learn."* Because learning is an active process, we can only learn by doing. Get the message? Dismiss your inhibitions and excuse yourself from other vacation obligations.

To Thine Own Self Be True

Your own initiative is essential. You can plan all the logistics of a trip, but it takes your personal desire and initiative to assure its success. If you allow yourself to be influenced by others and their likes and dislikes you are going to feel disillusioned. Possibly, you care nothing for art galleries or museums and for years have trudged wearily through places everyone tells you to go. Think about the things *you* have

---

*Dale Carnegie, How to Stop Worrying and Start Living (New York: Simon & Schuster, Inc., 1944), p 43.

always wanted to do. Be yourself and your honesty will pay big dividends.

A travel editor of a large eastern newspaper commented, "Above all, don't present the image of someone you aren't. Sooner or later it will foul you up." If you really don't enjoy sightseeing, touring and large groups of people, don't get caught up in that kind of a holiday. Your choice of vacation should be carefully thought out and first consideration given to your interests and pleasure.

The vacation traveler is motivated by the season, place and price. If your budget is a bit strained, take a mini-vacation and stay close to home. Pleasure cannot be measured by the distance one travels. It may be important to plan fewer days away and treat yourself to a super time rather than stretch the number of days and realize the trip was a bummer because of a tight budget. A personal philosophy I hold dear in travel is simply "Less is More" and it applies both to packing and to planning. Fewer days spent pleasurably are far superior to skimming by in second-rate rooms and riding public transit if you're the type who prefers hailing a taxi.

My personal idea of a "perfect" vacation close to home is to indulge myself for about three days at a health spa. Following the attention and rest of those marvelous days the entire world seems easy to conquer. The travel section of your Sunday newspaper will stir your imagination to numerous great mini-vacations. You will probably be surprised at the number of different holidays available, some within a few hundred miles of your home. There are resort facilities throughout the country featuring water sports at lakes and beaches; in the West there are guest ranches with horseback riding, cookouts and cowboys; other resorts feature tennis, golf, water or snow skiing with resident pros who are available to give instruction. Enjoy Broadway shows? Treat yourself to a Theater Tour of New York City—it comes as a complete package with hotel accommodations, transportation and show reservations. Or you might prefer to go steamboating on the Mississippi—trips vary from a three-day weekend holiday to an eleven-day round trip from New Orleans to Cincinnati. Above all, don't spend your vacation dollars flying to faraway places to look at historical sites that in all honesty bore you. Take the time to think it over and consider the alternatives.

My years of travel have taught me that people are equally as important as places in contributing to a memorable trip. A genuine curiosity about people, coupled with friendliness and a warm sense of humor, will make every trip an adventure. With a positive *attitude* every trip *is* an adventure and the world is limitless in opportunities. Replace negative thoughts with anticipation of new places and exciting new experiences and as you assume control you will grow in confidence. Focus on the moment and you will know good things are about to happen.

Several key words important to successful travel begin with the letter "A". *Attitude* heads the list and a close second is *awareness.* To be aware means making a conscious effort to actually look at and understand the surroundings and services available. The confidence you will feel as you learn to concentrate on being aware will become characteristic in the sense of mature responsibility that too often is dormant in a woman's life. The social role of the male has taught him from an early age to be aware of the area and the facilities around him. It is important to recognize the advantage of this faculty and how awareness is a learned habit that can be easily acquired.

Start practicing immediately. Stop for a moment to orient yourself in public areas. In parking garages you will see visuals for various street entrances and exits, elevators, escalators, restrooms, attendant and cashier. In depots and terminals there will be many additional signs to direct you to ticket counters, departure gates, baggage claim and ground transportation including buses, limousines, courtesy cars, and car rental counters. Here signs will be supported by public address announcements concerning various departure information. It is important to learn not only to look, but to see—not only to listen but to hear. With practice you will begin to assimilate that information which is of value to you, and simply dismiss the rest.

Another "A" word of great importance is *ask*. The expedient way of learning an answer to a question is to ask. Never allow shyness or embarrassment to take control of your life. Assume an assertive air with your fresh attitude about travel and be ready to ask lots of questions. People enjoy being helpful and questions start conversations that result in friendships.

Let's review the "A" words associated with travel. Attitude promises adventure. Awareness provides confidence. Asking eliminates confusion. A trip free of confusion and filled with confidence is certain to be an adventure. Keep reading, we have only just begun!

During my early training in airline school, an instructor provided this visual description to the class. She picked up an ordinary, medium-sized suitcase and said, "I want each of you to pack a suitcase with your troubles and worries. Leave that case at home and board your aircraft free of any problems and cares."

I share this personal lesson because it taught me early the wisdom of those three simple words—"peace of mind." You can insure your travel pleasure by taking the steps necessary to enjoy the composure, confidence and general feeling of well-being that can only come from peace of mind.

As any seasoned traveler knows, the success of a delightful vacation or productive business meeting depends to a large degree on *planning*. Homework completed before your trip obviously includes the large decisions such as transportation, lodging and finances. However, it is often the small details which can make the difference between pleasure and discomfort that are oftentimes overlooked. You are a special person with personal and individual needs whether you are traveling alone or vacationing with a friend, husband or children. It is imperative that details be handled and responsibilities delegated so that when you are ready to leave you can do so and enjoy your trip with "peace of mind."

A woman is in control when she understands a few fundamentals concerning the where, why, and when of travel. There are three important things to consider in planning a trip. They are cost, comfort and convenience. Divide a sheet of paper into three columns. Write "cost" at the top of the first, "comfort" at the top of the second and "convenience" at the top of the third. Under these columns jot down notes for consideration in each category. The result is a skeleton outline to help you plan wisely and avoid mistakes. The savings in time and dollars will provide extra dividends on your trip.

Consider the cost column. If this is a business trip you will know which items can be considered business expenses. If it is strictly vacation you may be one of the fortunate ones who has already budgeted and know the exact amount of money available for the trip. However, for many it may be necessary to estimate the approximate amount and plan to save it before the time arrives. Planning early helps to provide that extra incentive necessary to budget and save for a specific goal.

As you move toward the comfort column, do consider the type of vacation you want. Too often, comfort is overlooked in the quest to fit a package into a given number of days at a given price. Will your emphasis be on the luxury of a first-class resort hotel? You may want to choose a closer destination to pay for the pleasure of your luxury.

On the other hand, for the back-to-nature lover, a rough-hewn lakeshore cottage with swimming, fishing and water sports all within a stone's throw may provide the comfort and the convenience at a cost that is well worth the price. Think seriously about your priorities. Reviewing this column carefully may provide the answer to why other trips have seemed to be lacking.

Now for the third column: convenience. This will provide

even more answers. There are so many choices and yet the person you are will determine the manner in which you interpret convenience. Do you always drive on your vacation? Is your time limited, and, if so, would it be worth the extra money to fly? Only by air can the miles become minutes and time is a precious resource that can never be recaptured. Or is air travel your only experience? If that is the case, consider resorts and vacation facilities accessible by motor coach or train. Perhaps you are dreaming of a cruise—absolute luxury!

Convenience should also take into consideration the location of your hotel, motel, or other lodging. How far are the beach, shops or "the action spots?" Don't spend the money you save on your room for taxis. The written exercise is to guide you in making major decisions. Take a few minutes to concentrate on the realities, perhaps daydream a bit, and then collect your thoughts. This is an important first step.

If you are thinking of something fairly close to home, check the newspaper travel section for ideas and also the classified section for vacation rentals. More and more people are acquiring condominiums and cabins in resort areas. Owners frequently offer them as rentals and they provide many of the comforts of home but are located in prime vacation or recreation areas.

When you plan trips involving greater distances, particularly other countries, you will most likely need the expertise of someone thoroughly familiar with all types of travel. The professional travel agent is your answer.

Travel Agents

Why do you need a travel agent? For exactly the same reasons you turn to an insurance broker or an attorney when you need expert help—to avoid costly errors and to take advantage of the benefits which only a professional can provide. Their services to you are paid for by the transportation industry in the form of commissions. Travel is big business and they are eager for you, their customer, to plan trips, take trips, and to enjoy trips so that you will come back to book more and bigger trips in the future.

Before you select a travel advisor, do your homework and fill in the columns on cost, comfort and convenience to the degree you can yourself. Visit your local library for some personal research on the areas you are considering. You may wish to consider several different options. If you are planning a trip to foreign countries take time to carefully study a map of each (or make a copy of it to take with you to the travel agent), memorize names of major cities and airports and in general familiarize yourself as much as possible with the climate, the people and the characteristics of the country. The agent will provide you with additional and more detailed information but this investment of your time is important and will allow you to share intelligently in the conversation with your travel agent. It will also help him or her to be more sensitive to your likes and dislikes in the planning of your trip.

If you have selected wisely, the agent will enjoy the search for your "dream vacation" every bit as much as you. He or she is a skilled counselor and your eagerness to learn makes you a perfect audience. I believe the prerequisite of a superb agent must be a light touch of theatrics—such a delight when the imagination can be stroked and ignited with stories about and descriptions of places to explore and moments to cherish.

And wherever do you find such an agent? Personal recommendation is excellent. Yellow pages offer an easy directory but be certain to look for the ASTA or the CTC seal. This endorsement indicates their membership in the American Society of Travel Agents and the Certified Travel Counselors respectively. A good agent will understand your needs and since they must travel extensively on business, you will benefit from their experience. Because you are a woman, you may find a woman travel agent will understand your particular needs better. Consider this when you are searching for an agent and don't rush your decision. You will probably talk with several before you find the one with whom you feel a mutual rapport. It is an investment of your time that is well worthwhile. Excellent advice on currency, clothes, climate, restaurants, hotels, shopping, bargains, local customs, tours, and countless other questions can be answered immediately by the qualified agent you select.

You may be steered to a delightful little hideaway hotel instead of the huge chain operation that makes it necessary to check the stationery in the room to know which country you are visiting. Hotel brochures can look very similar and you deserve the charm and caring that is part of the choice places available—but only if you know about them. Because travel today has become complicated and confusing to everyone, the agent who makes it his business to stay alert to the changes is your best choice. Work closely with her and be sure to share your likes—even more important, your dislikes. Too often priorities seem to be slanted toward the things to do. Do not overlook the things you do not want to do and say it loud and clear to your agent.

Off Season

Consider a resort holiday "off season" as opposed to going to a particular spot at the height of its tourist season. The benefits are special—fewer crowds, better service, less expensive and the opportunity of meeting sharp people who think the way you do.

Package Tours

You will undoubtedly hear the term "package tour" as you begin talking with travel agents. A package tour may contain round trip air fare, hotel accommodations, transportation to and from the airport and come with or without meals included in the price. Often the same package tour includes sightseeing tours, or they may be an "add on" option to be booked separately. The contents of package tours vary. Do not hesitate to ask questions when you are uncertain of terms, fares, tours or anything else that requires explanation.

You will also find some "package tours" which contain only air arrangements. Land portions, including accommodations, are additional. You may consider booking the "tour portion" and selecting only the bits and pieces of the itinerary that appeal to you. The savings is often substantial and you will enjoy the best of two worlds. You are not expected to read and digest the volumes of printed material that is available to the potential traveler. The fares, selections, and best buys change daily and only an individual in the travel business can hope to keep current on the subject.

Emergency Travel

The moment you must travel in a hurry—Go by Air! If time permits place the full arrangements for your trip in the hands of a travel agent. If the emergency occurs at night or on a Sunday and you must phone direct to the airline, it is helpful to ask for the supervisor on duty. That person's seniority and experience will be valuable in providing you with quick, clear and competent service. The supervisor is in a position to offer additional assistance such as, for example, to teletype ahead to find out what transportation is available if the airport is not within easy access or your final destination. Be sure to explain that it is an emergency. Tell the supervisor your destination and the date and time you can be ready to leave. If possible, make a reservation for your return trip to avoid problems in obtaining a flight home. If necessary it can be charged later.

An important conclusion to any phone reservation is to confirm where you plan to pick up your ticket. It is best to stop by a ticket counter before going to the airport and thus avoid any long lines or a last-minute rush. However, in an emergency it may be impossible to do so. In that case, ask for the ticket to be prepared and you will pick it up at the airport. When you do arrive at the terminal, ask for the Passenger Service Manager on duty. This individual is specially trained to help in emergency travel. Do not hesitate to explain your priorities and exactly how the airline can best help you. This may be in preboarding or asking that the flight attendants be alerted to your problem. In the event you have an invalid or handicapped person to take from one city to another, the airlines provide exceptional help and service to make the trip as comfortable and convenient as possible. Any emergency should be brought to the attention of the airline's personnel—you will find them eager and willing to help in any way they can.

Club Mediterranee

Excitement and fun and a gem of an idea. Your travel agent can fill you in on the specific details. For a condensed explanation, hold on—before you finish reading, you will probably be on your way to the nearest office.

The following appeared in the March 1976 issue of *Harper's Bazaar*. "The surest way to avoid the pains of single vacations while reveling in their pleasures is Club Mediterranee. An international network of seventy resorts with twenty tailored to American tastes, it offers an informal environment of casual dressing, easy acquaintanceships, secluded activities and instruction varying from yoga to snorkeling, sailing and tennis."

The basic structure of the Club Med (the shorter way of describing same and used by all in the travel industry) appeals to the adventurous traveler willing to double up with another guest (same sex) and trade the conservative privacy of the traditional room and bath for the pleasure of companionship.

Guests do not carry money at the Club Med. Your prepayment covers food and lodging. A string of poppet beads are purchased upon arrival and these are worn around your wrist, neck or general anatomy. Thirsty? Merely unsnap a bead in exchange for a rum punch.

The guests frequenting the resorts are generally between the ages of twenty-four and forty. Favorites for Americans are those spots in Guadeloupe, Martinique, Tahiti, Hawaii, Playa Blanca and Cancun in Mexico.

"Patterned after the original idea started by Gerald Blitz, the Belgian diamond cutter who bought up U.S. Army supply tents and put them to logical use at a campsite in Majorca for impecunious but adventurous young Parisians, the Club steers the American traveler to villages with bilingual staffs and amenities, like air conditioning and private indoor plumbing."

So much more can be said about this unique alternative vacation. A personal reference from someone who has recently completed a Club Mediterranee holiday is an excellent source. And in case you are wondering, yes, it is okay if you are married and, yes, you can share the room with your husband.

Cruise Travel

Have you placed "cruise" under both the comfort and convenience columns? That's exactly where I put cruise travel. A cruise ship has been described as a "floating hotel." The Cunard steamship line has used an appropriate slogan, "Getting there is half the fun" and so it is in the memories of many who enjoy ship travel. As a general rule the longer cruises attract an older age group and the weekend trip to seven-day trips cater to a younger crowd. You might wish to consider the coast of Mexico or a Caribbean cruise. Without rushing to meet deadlines, you can go ashore for a few hours and return to enjoy the rest of the day in the ship's swimming pool or reading. The fine opportunity of seeing a little of each place allows you to consider returning at another time for a longer visit. A distinct advantage of living on the ship is the enormous convenience for anyone who dislikes packing and unpacking and moving from hotel to hotel.

When you start considering all the various holidays available, be alert to the many questions that are never answered in the tour folder. Advertising copy is designed to "sell" by appealing to your first impulse. Notice how you immediately feel positive about an attractive color brochure and a well-written description of the facilities?

Look beyond the gloss and glitter of a sales campaign and into the areas that really affect you. The behind-the-scenes truth can tell you a great deal. Does the resort cater to conventions? Will you be sandwiched between hundreds of pleasure-seeking tourists and spend precious vacation hours waiting for a tennis court or a tee-off time that is hours into the heat of the day? Hotel and food service is delayed when an over abundance of guests are demanding attention. Don't be misled by the exterior packaging—the contents may prove to be a nightmare.

"So where do I go for *inside* information?" The answer is in asking questions—lots of questions and of many people. Glean information from friends who have been to various areas, your professional travel agent, and if the resort is nearby or lists a toll free number, call with a list of specific questions about their facilities and accommodations. This will help to avoid many of the surprises that can prove less than pleasurable. I am reminded of the Holiday Inn's sensible advertising: "The best surprise is no surprise." Of course, we would want only to apply their slogan to the comfort of the room and surroundings. The many surprises that are characteristic of and a delight each and every day of your trip are one of the great enticements of travel.

Two

ORGANIZATION

Any trip worth taking deserves your planning time, but when the clutter of brochures, maps, literature and books starts to take over, planning can get in the way of progress. A trip diary is the solution.

Personal Trip Diary

Gather all the literature you have been collecting, the maps, brochures and notes together in one place. You probably have enough to fill a small, or perhaps a large, suitcase. That space is very precious and the weight can become a real burden. Carefully look over each brochure and usually you will find one paragraph, a single page, sometimes only one restaurant suggestion is all that interests you. Without hesitation, tear the page out and chuck the rest. Continue tearing and clipping, saving only those things you will use. This organization of your travel materials may take a half-hour or perhaps an hour. When you have the essential items together, you are ready to start putting together your Personal Trip Diary.

For years, the type of report folder having three brads and two pockets has worked best for me. They are inexpensive and available in all stationery or variety stores. Color coding is a clear and very effective way to know at a glance the information you want. Use construction paper and a paper punch to prepare the pages to fit the three brads of the report folder.

You may wish to use one color on which to Scotch tape information on various activities available in the area you are going to visit; on another color, restaurants and shows that will be playing there; a third color could contain various purchases for yourself or gifts you wish to look for on your trip. Or, if you are on your way to Europe, orange sheets might contain information about France, green sheets for Spain, and blue for Italy. I keep basic information on white, and several additional sheets are always kept available in the folder.

Let us assume you have already spent an hour sorting just the essential material you will take for reference and also that you have decided to give my style of report folder a try. Now use the hole puncher again for materials of a size that will go directly into the folder, and Scotch tape the smaller pieces to the colored construction paper. If you need only one section of a large and cumbersome map, cut away only that portion and secure it in the folder. The two pockets of the report folder are convenient; however, keep them free for use on the trip. Take a legal size envelope and staple or tape it securely to the inside cover. This provides an excellent place to keep tour ticket receipts, business cards you receive from those you meet on the trip, the names and addresses of restaurants and boutiques you hear are special. Think about the times someone has given you the name of a great little restaurant or a place to buy fine leather goods that is unknown to many. What happened to the slip of paper on which you jotted down the information? With a personal trip diary the answer is always the same. The information is in your diary.

An extremely important piece of information to place in the diary is a list which includes your passport number, certificate of registration numbers, traveler's check numbers, medical prescriptions, physician's phone number, insurance policy numbers and any phone numbers you may need while on vacation. Knowing all of this information is in one place and with you at all times will give you the peace of mind we spoke of earlier.

I encourage you to assemble this trip diary early in the planning stages of your trip. As you receive more literature, you can decide whether you will take it along or just copy some highlights and discard the rest. Keep a list of the things you must pick up, or deliver, before you leave and clip it inside your folder. This checklist will become a visual discipline that will keep you enthusiastic about your progress. When countless small things are tugging at your memory, it is easy to forget and to be caught up in a frustrating last-minute deadline which will result in exhaustion before you ever start the trip. Don't let that happen to you. The trip diary is an excellent beginning.

But your trip diary doesn't stop here. You will find it *really* starts to work for you the moment you begin your holiday. As you share conversation with your seat partner or others you meet, be alert for their suggestions and names of places that are special. Place the information directly on the pages of your diary to avoid having to deal with small pieces of paper. The frustration of misplaced information will be a thing of the past. Each day will start with the freedom of knowing you have not forgotten anything. The addresses, phone numbers, maps, guides, tour tickets, and vital information will be in your trip diary and can be slipped into your tote bag with camera, traveler's checks, and a few personal items for the day. You may find you will convert others along the way as they see how it works.

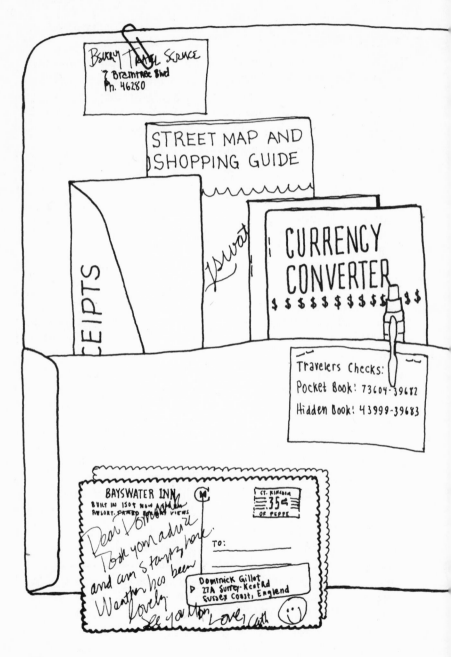

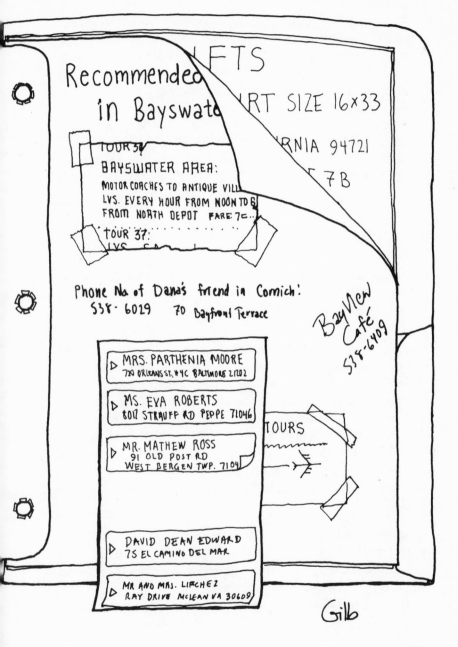

Gilb

Returning from your trip, the full report can be placed in a vacation file box. When a friend or business associate mentions planning a trip to the same area, you can reach for your file and hand the entire collection over so they can profit from your pioneering efforts and discoveries.

We have devoted an entire chapter to International Travel; however, certain items require advance handling and those are included here. Some things can wait until the last minute, others cannot. Travel Editor Georgia Hesse tells her readers in her popular travel guide, *Going My Way,* "Wherever and however you go, your papers must be in order."

Checklist

This has been prepared to help you put your papers in order early. You'll be glad you did! Make notes in your trip diary of when and where you will apply for each of these items.

Passport　Apply at the passport agency if you live in San Francisco, Boston, Chicago, Los Angeles, Honolulu, New York City, New Orleans, Miami, Philadelphia, Seattle, or Washington, D.C. County courthouses and some U.S. post offices are also authorized to accept passport applications. You will need proof of your citizenship (birth certificate is good) and two passport photos, personal identification and the money to pay for the passport. It is a good idea to have several extra passport photographs because you may need them.

Visas and Tourist Cards　These are not required for all foreign travel—such as in Western Europe where a passport alone is sufficient. Visas are required to enter most countries in Africa, the Middle East and the Orient.

It is important to know that a visa is not a document, but

rather it is an official stamp in your passport, which means if you need visas for three countries your passport must go to each consulate to be stamped. If you live away from those consulates, your travel agent will have to mail it to each consulate in Washington, D.C. This will take at least a week before it is back, and then it must be sent off once again. The important point here is to be sure to allow your agent enough time to obtain your necessary travel authorizations.

Tourist cards are required in Mexico and a number of countries in South America. Unlike a visa, this is a separate document and does not require that your passport accompany the request. There are frequent changes in the requirements and it is necessary for the professional travel agent to repeatedly check on them, so allow sufficient time.

International Certificate of Vaccination Check with your travel agent concerning which vaccinations are required depending on which countries you plan to visit. Have your shots well in advance of the trip. These can be obtained from your personal physician, or, in some areas, from county health clinics at a fraction of the normal fee.

International Driving Permit If you plan to drive, apply. Permits are issued by the American Automobile Association and the National Automobile Club. The permit is valid for one year from the date of departure and the cost is $3.00. It will be necessary to present two photographs (passport type).

Certificate of Registration of Ownership You may obtain registration certificates at U.S. customs offices. Take the articles you wish to register (cameras, jewelry, watches, furs, etc.) with you when you apply. The registration will allow you to return from abroad without having to pay duty on items that were in your possession when you departed. Should you not live in an area convenient to a customs office, take any proof of ownership of valuable items with you—such as the sales receipt, jeweler's appraisal or insurance policy.

Tip-Packs, Pre-Packs or Pocket Money Packs This convenient item is a prepackaged envelope of foreign currency in small denominations. The amount varies from $10 to $20 or $50. You can familiarize yourself with small bills and coins before the trip and have them immediately available for tips, taxis, and the other needs when you arrive in a foreign country. This package will cost a bit more; however, the advance practice it gives you is a worthwhile investment. I would suggest you consider additional amounts if you are planning to arrive in a country on a weekend when the banks and American Express offices are closed. To stand in line for an exchange of U.S. cash or traveler's checks is tiring after a long trip.

You can avoid this by picking up enough foreign currency to meet your needs until you can use the services of a bank. The hotel will provide an exchange; however, there is a service charge and you will save money by using a bank overseas or taking traveler's checks in the currency of the country you are visiting.

This is possible before your trip by asking your own bank to obtain foreign traveler's checks for you. Give them advance notice and project ahead the amount you will need. Remember that every time you make an exchange you pay a commission. Also remember that all foreign currencies can be exchanged again when you return home.

Traveler's Checks Before buying traveler's checks, ask the advice of your travel agent concerning the brand name and the amounts in which to buy them. Not all traveler's checks are readily accepted *all over the world.* Additionally, find out how quickly they can be refunded if lost or stolen while you are out of the country. Can you get your money back while you are there or do you have to wait until you return to the United States? You will find traveler's checks available from your bank, savings and loan or other financial institution. Do pick them up fairly early to avoid a last-minute detail, but do *not* start spending them until you are on your way.

You may wish to try my fun bookkeeping system for travel abroad. Decide the amount of money you can spend in each city, and write the name in pencil on the back of the traveler's checks. When you are about to leave one place to go to another, you may find you would like to buy a few additional things; however, the concern is whether or not you will have enough money left for the remaining stops on your trip. Perhaps you are leaving Paris for Rome. If the next traveler's check indicates Paris, you are safe in buying the French perfume or other item. Occasionally, it may be necessary to borrow from one city to spend in another; however, the system does eliminate a lot of budget keeping. As you spend a check, turn to your list of numbers in your trip diary and jot the date and expenditure opposite the number for an accurate record of your budget.

Following are details which should receive your attention whether you are traveling within or out of the country.

Medic Alert   If you have a heart condition, allergy to penicillin, asthma, epilepsy, or any other medical problem, membership in Medic Alert will provide a bracelet that identifies your medical condition. Write the Medic Alert Foundation, Turlock, California, 95380, for a brochure.

Prescriptions   Take along a supply of any medicines you regularly need and ask your doctor for an extra copy of the written prescriptions to carry with you in your trip diary.

Eyeglasses or Contact Lenses   If at all possible, it is wise to pack an extra pair of glasses or contact lenses in the event yours are lost or broken. If you have been planning to buy a pair of prescription sunglasses, do order them in time for your trip.

Business Cards If you already have your own business cards, fine. You know their value. If not, I urge you to run, not walk, to the nearest commercial printer and order a supply. You may or may not wish to include your address and phone number—you may wish to use an avocation as identification (Quilt Maker, Pianist, Designer) or if you feel like being mysterious—use only your name. Put some thought into the impression you want to create with your card. A commercial printer will be able to show you samples and help you to select an appropriate type and style, and if you wish, a logo.

I strongly advocate that all women have business cards with them at all times, not just when traveling. When on a trip it will not only provide proper spelling of your name and address for the shopkeeper whom you have asked to mail a parcel to your home, but it looks much more professional anytime you are making reservations for a rental car, tour or anything that requires identification. Order them now.

Address Labels Before you leave, address self-adhesive labels to those you will want to send letters or postcards while you are gone. Slip them into the envelope in your trip diary. Dropping a few lines to friends, relatives and business contacts is much easier to do when this small chore is completed beforehand. In addition to saving vacation time, it also alleviates the need for carrying a cumbersome address book.

Home Care

This may require very little attention or a great deal. The woman who must provide for child care, home maintenance and other services during her absence is going to need plenty of lead time to complete these arrangements. If your status is that of a single woman living in an apartment building, you may find a phone call to your landlord or manager and stopping the newspaper are all that is necessary.

Another's obligations may be incredibly extensive by comparison. A last minute dash—hoping something has not been overlooked can prove exhausting and you will start your trip with confusion and anxiety. In *Everywoman's Guide to Time Management** I suggest compiling a permanent Household Instruction Booklet that covers all areas of concern in complete detail. Once it is done it can simply be updated when necessary. It is particularly valuable in the event of an emergency when you can simply hand it to whoever will be taking care of those matters for you.

Provide copies of your itinerary for the office, your neighbors and your relatives. At this time, also take the full list of traveler's checks and give a copy to close friends at home. You may need the information and this duplication of numbers is good insurance.

Every woman lives with her personal obligations daily and other arrangements are necessary before a trip can be a reality. The best plan to follow in arranging for time away from your home is to do it well in advance. This will provide you with that all-important *peace of mind,* knowing your responsibilities for the family and other obligations have been taken care of long before you leave.

Personal Grooming

In my time management classes, there is session called *Sparkle Your Self-Image.* The purpose is to show women the importance of allowing personal time for a maintenance program in good grooming. The principles of self-care are even more important before and during a trip.

---

*Les Femmes, 1977.

If your hair style requires regular permanents, schedule one about two weeks before leaving. The lead time will allow soft manageable hair during your time away. A good haircut about a week before leaving can mean easy care for the blow-dry cuts that are so fashionable now. An additional word on hair is offered from my experience in many years' travel. If you enjoy it, treat yourself to beauty salon luxuries during your holiday. You deserve the comfort and atmosphere specially designed to indulge a woman.

If you tend to be even slightly overweight it somehow seems easier to take off those few extra pounds when you have a very specific deadline in mind. Try eating a little less at each meal. Keep nutrition carefully balanced rather than going on a fad diet which may leave you pounds lighter but physically depleted. Changing habits is helpful. If you have lunch regularly at restaurants, try taking a lunch—low in calories and high in nutrition—and eat in a nearby park with a friend or good book for company. Not only will this result in sending you on your holiday feeling slightly svelte and good about yourself, but the savings can help those vacation dollars grow. A word of advice—this is not a bad idea even if you are at your perfect weight—particularly if you are going on a cruise or to visit friends or relatives who judge their own hospitality by the richness and quantity of the food they serve. You'll find it a lot easier to drop a few pounds below your normal weight in the weeks before you leave than to take it off after you return home.

Comfortable clothing always requires advance planning. Do not, under any circumstances buy new shoes or undergarments and wear them for the first time while traveling. Clothing should fit comfortably. A bra that rides up, a bikini panty with too-tight elastic around the leg, knee hi's that cut off circulation at the calf or hose that will not allow room for toe wiggling can be pure misery. A blister resulting from wearing a pair of shoes just one day, or even a few hours, can continue to be a problem even when you return to a normally comfortable pair of shoes. Don't take the chance; buy and be sure you have sufficient, comfortable shoes and clothes weeks in advance.

Travel Treasures

I have a very special friend who is a seasoned traveler. She selects a special portion of a dresser drawer in which to gather and keep "travel treasures," the little things bought or saved especially for a future trip. In addition to being vitally important when you are ready to start packing your suitcase, these treasures also add incentive and excitement as you prepare for your trip.

If you need to purchase a travel cosmetic case, do select a practical, plastic lined bag that will hold a lot but take up the smallest possible space. Shop for this item early. Collecting toiletry items that travel well is an art. Never make the mistake of dropping a large and economy size of anything into your travel case. Transfer from large bottles to small, plastic bottles or jars. Things to "tuck away" are sample sizes of your favorite lotions, shampoo, and other toiletries. They are travel perfect in small but adequate sizes. For these items leisure shopping is the most practical. Somehow last minute searches seldom uncover exactly what you want to take along.

An inexpensive item which I feel is indispensible is a good pair of comfortable earplugs. Getting proper rest is vital while you are traveling and noises such as street traffic or early morning activity outside your door or window can be extremely annoying. The only truly comfortable earplugs I have found are made of beeswax and since I have located only one source I have included it in the Resource List.

Following are some additional items you may want to collect and have ready. An elastic clothes line requires little space but is exceptionally handy for your drip-dry washables when placed over the tub. A few of the inflatable hangers sold in notions departments are far preferable to the wooden hangers most hotels place in their closets. Your fragile and delicate garments will not snag and they dry easier on the plastic hangers. There is also the dual purpose of using one as a bath pillow. When not in use, deflate and slip into your cosmetic case. Pick up a travel-size sewing kit containing a cloth tape measure, safety pins, buttons and even a needle threader at a notion's counter. It will prove invaluable.

Probably the most seasoned traveler whom I interviewed makes frequent short business trips to give one-day seminars on college campuses or to social organizations. Her treasures include a small three-way stand-up picture frame with photographs of her husband and two sons. She was eager to share her travel experiences. Although she thoroughly enjoys her short trips, the very first thing she does upon arriving in her hotel room, she confided, is to rearrange the furniture. If there is a small desk she prefers to move it out and turn it around from a corner so that she can work at it facing the room rather than a wall. She likes to have the usual one comfortable chair near the window with the good reading lamp next to it.

In addition to the family photo, this expert traveler enjoys picking up a small bouquet of flowers to brighten her room. She often finds them, she went on to explain, right in the produce department of the grocery store she always seeks out in order to buy some fresh fruit for her room. This provides a healthy early morning snack to stave off starvation until she is ready to go down to breakfast. In case you are wondering, as I was, if she carries a flower vase around with her, the answer is no. A glass from the bathroom wrapped in the green tissue from around the bouquet and held in place with a rubber band is sufficient.

I enthusiastically agree with her idea of buying fresh fruit for her room. When you find yourself suddenly hungry it is so easy to pick up junk food which can raise total havoc with your stomach, detract from your pleasure at mealtime and sabotage your figure.

Like my friend and her "travel treasures" I collect continually. It supports my motto, "Have bag—will travel." Over the years I have picked up some innovative ideas to assure comfort in new surroundings.

At the top of my list is a 100-watt light bulb which I pack in the corrugated cardboard it comes in and travels inside a shoe. It has been my experience that hotel bedside lamps frequently do not provide adequate light to support my habit of reading in bed.

Following a busy or hectic day of sightseeing, a refreshing cup of bouillon is absolutely perfect. A small electric coil will heat water for tea, coffee or soup. Pick one up at a drug store or notions department. It's a life saver if you like your coffee *while* you're getting dressed.

Avoid taking too many packets and gadgets however, since even the smallest of things will take up space; for example, don't take foil travel packets of shoe polish if you never use polish at home. You can buy packets that promise spot removal, but club soda serves as an instant spot remover and is usually available in your hotel. A bar of soap is fine for most washable items, or possibly you may want to transfer liquid soap into a plastic travel bottle for hand laundry. An umbrella that folds to a small size is great for those who use umbrellas at home, but if you are not an umbrella user, a trip is not going to convert you, so leave it at home. To alert yourself against being a victim of taking far too much, just ask the two words "Why" and "When" of each item and your answer will tell you if it is worth space in your case.

Be sure to pack a travel alarm clock. If you don't have one, consider purchasing this item in a duty-free shop.

Memories of holiday purchases add to the pleasure every time you use them. My son remembers the large selection of travel clocks in London and how we purchased both a travel alarm clock and a small watch for him at the elegant and prestigious Harrod's.

Another must for travel is dental floss. In addition to its intended purpose of dental hygiene, it will also become an instant heavy-duty thread in case of an emergency. Perfect for the shank button that keeps popping off a favorite suit or jacket.

An individualized pill case is far more convenient than single bottles of this and that. The few minutes it takes to organize these things results in your taking less and saving time, space and energy.

I always carry an emergency "baggie" containing a number of bandaids, the pillbox mentioned above for aspirin and any necessary prescriptions, a few wash-and-dry packets, a small blunt-end scissors (priceless) and a "real" spoon. I prefer a simple stainless steel spoon (rather than the plastic or wooden substitutes) for eating a carton of yogurt or ice cream when I have the urge for an impromptu snack. Be sure to include a roll of transparent tape to repair a hemline that has let you down at just the moment you are late; use it to reinforce packages, wrap a special gift, remove lint (wrap a few strips around four fingers and stroke the garment gently) or countless other uses you will discover along the way.

Do not be concerned about little items which can be picked up in local pharmacies and grocery stores which are available almost everywhere. A valuable lesson of travel is that it teaches you, if you let it, how other people live. Among the most instructive pursuits in a foreign land is to foray into the neighborhood pharmacy, department store or the corner grocery.

Another convenient item is a tiny flashlight that can be kept handy in your purse and placed next to the bed each evening. A strange hotel room can become frightening if you cannot find the light switch at night. A ballpoint pen with its own light proves handy when you need to read a menu or sign a credit card receipt in a dimly lit restaurant, or jot a note in a theater or movie.

I have used the same small, soft-rolled velvet jewel case for years. Not only are my favorite pieces of jewelry kept safe, but a few folded up bills and often my traveler's checks are slipped into this roll. It is carried in my handbag, and the peace of mind is in knowing it is not in the hotel room or a piece of luggage.

Take a look at the luggage tags on suitcases the next time you travel. It will surprise you how few good looking personalized tags are around. You may wish to order your own handsome luggage tags in advance of your next trip. Airport security suggests using the type that is encased with a cover to hide your name and address. Some recent burglaries have been traced to the thief who purposefully checked out the name tags of outgoing luggage and set about to burglarize the home during the absence of the residents.

A further precaution against any misplaced luggage is to have your name, address and itinerary on a card taped to the inside of the case. Often the luggage can be sent directly to you when it has been retrieved if this information is in the suitcase.

Contacts

It is up to you to make the contacts and this is where your own initiative is of utmost importance to you. If you simply buy your tickets and go, hoping strangers will make your trip an adventure, you are in for a disappointment. But on the other hand, if you lay some groundwork, you will not only increase the odds but may be absolutely amazed at what develops.

Do not run away from your job, hobbies or your associations when planning a trip. The association you have with certain companies, businesses and organizations can provide valuable contacts that will lead to real in-depth pleasure in your travel. I like what Jean Baer, author of *Follow Me,* says: "Any woman regardless of age, appearance, occupation, or economic status can meet people abroad if she embarks on an intensive homework program before she leaves her own front door."

Perhaps the company you work for has offices in other parts of the United States or the world. A letter sent in advance, possibly a letter of introduction from your immediate superior, may open doors to those with whom you have a great deal in common.

Review the organizations to which you belong. List the contacts you have at home and don't forget clubs, church and school. Many times I have been in a strange city and attended a church service and joined in the coffee hour of hospitality that often follows. Church members are exceptionally friendly and eager to make a stranger feel at home. It is a wonderful opportunity to share some time with members of your faith. You will make personal contacts who will be happy to tell you about other activities happening in the city and share their knowledge of favorite local interests in an atmosphere of genuine warmth and friendship.

Whatever affiliations you have can serve to open many doors with a bit of preplanning. How about membership in national organizations, such as the International Federation of Business and Professional Women's Clubs or the Soroptomist International Association. Should time slip away and letters not be sent before leaving, call when you arrive. The local number will be listed for chapters, organizations, and service groups. Ask for the president, explain briefly who you are and your affiliation with the organization.

Perhaps you are a journalist—call the local press club. Nursing—related organizations and your colleagues are everywhere. The college woman shouldn't overlook eligibility for membership in the American Association of University Women. How about Scout leader? If you are one who spent many years working with little acknowledgment, and even though it is now a dim memory, a long overdue award may be yours. Look up the chapter in the city you are visiting and don't overlook the foreign chapters. They will be delighted to invite you as a visitor to an upcoming meeting or local outing, and if none are scheduled, just sharing the time chatting on the phone will provide many leads for special points of interest and activities you would not have known about without personal recommendations. Service groups attract the type of member who is eager and willing to help. Never hesitate to ask for help because people automatically respond when they feel needed.

One of your friends, neighbors or relatives may suggest you call on their friends while you are visiting their city. A personal letter may be mailed prior to your arrival and will alert those you may be calling. Give the date and time of arrival in their city and the place you will be staying.

Now, imagine you have arrived in Miami, settled comfortably in your hotel and would like some personal recommendations from one who lives in the city. Look in your trip diary for the address and phone number of your friend's friend and pick up the phone to call her. Explain who you are and extend greetings to her from your mutual friend. Have some simple questions concerning the city and general information ready. You will quickly be able to tell if your call was anticipated and your contact eager to share her knowledge and perhaps meet you for lunch. Or, if your call has come at an inconvenient time, you can ask a question or two and will still leave her feeling she has been of help to you if only to recommend her favorite restaurant or tell you the best store in which to look for a specific purchase.

Occasionally you may run into those who are indeed so delighted to meet you and so eager to be hospitable that they tend to take over all your time. It is wise to indicate that you do have some plans, which you need not explain. This will allow you the privacy and freedom to pursue other activities.

Memorable experiences will be yours when you show a lively curiosity about places and people. Speaking from personal experience, the hospitality and warmth of friends of friends, contacts through jobs, hobbies and social or service organizations, will open avenues that would otherwise have forever remained unexplored.

"Ask not what to pack, but what not to pack."

Three

PACKING

We've come a long way since the fifties when the heavy set of matched luggage was the favorite graduation gift. You can still see those cases, built to last a lifetime, burdensome and archaic. To compound the problem, many people overpack and then hate every minute they must wait, resent every dollar they must tip, and proceed to strain their backs and their dispositions as they lug and tug their impersonal and overweight suitcases.

Minutes quickly add up to hours of lost time when it is spent waiting in baggage claim areas. Plans to take an impromptu side trip are frequently cancelled (or never even considered) because the luggage presents a problem. Envision a sarcastic-looking face painted on any suitcase that is pushing you around. The suitcase, or even worse, the plural suitcases can rob you of the very mobility and freedom that you set out to find in the first place.

Suitcase Selection

Today travel cases come in styles, shapes and sizes to suit every purpose, preference and pocketbook. The popular casual dress habits and fabulous new fabrics have given us license to pack *less* and actually have *more*. A multitude of different and delightful cases are available, as a visit to any large luggage store or department will reveal. Some of the newest bags are actually enormous shoulder totes that expand to accommodate a weekend wardrobe. Most major manufacturers have a version of this innovative bag— unusual, but probably not for everyone. The popular soft-sided cases allow a tremendous amount of flexibility, are much easier to handle and are very durable. Manufacturers are responding to the needs of the traveling public who realize the convenience of light luggage. Also, the quick, collapsible sets of wheels for comfortably towing a large bag are readily available. One thing is certain—heavy and bulky suitcases are a thing of the past.

When shopping for travel cases or bags be sure to look in children's departments at the wide range of suitcases, carpet bags and canvas duffle bags that are available. You will be delighted with the sizes and styles in fabric and vinyl. They are light as a feather, a joy to use and usually very reasonably priced. Don't overlook the discount houses, the department stores and the specialty shops either. The search is great fun and the choices varied and plentiful.

It is important to take the right size case for the trip. Start with a small and lightweight case that you can easily carry. This should be a bag which can fit under your airplane seat or in an overhead rack on a bus or train. Airlines generally specify forty-five inches as the maximum size for a carry-on bag. This is measured by adding the length to the width to the height. A typical example would be a case twenty-three inches long, thirteen inches wide and nine inches high which totals exactly forty-five inches. The size limitation also helps to control the impulse to overpack.

For longer trips which will require more luggage you may wish to have a sixty-inch case, or the approximate equivalent. This will hold many changes of clothing, other shoes, handbags and nonessential sundries. Apart from this, it is always a good idea to pack at least one comfortable and complete change of clothing, all necessary toiletries and cosmetics in your carry-on bag in the event you are temporarily unable to get into the larger case. Regardless of whether you are traveling by train, motor coach or plane you will probably want to check the large piece of luggage through to your destination and live out of the smaller bag until you catch up with it again. Or, you may wish to put the larger case in a locker at a depot or terminal in order to take a short side trip. It will, in effect, become a portable closet, out of which you can pack a daily tote bag or select a condensed wardrobe in order to travel light and easy for an overnight or weekend side trip. If you are checking out of your room for a night or two, you will find most hotels have locked storage facilities where they will hold your luggage as a courtesy for their guests.

We have discussed a rather typical pair of suitcases, which should, when properly packed, take you almost anywhere. But don't feel limited to these. Perhaps you would travel more freely with an ordinary cosmetic shoulder bag for your essentials and take a colorful and modern version of the old valet (or hanging) bag and keep your clothes on their hangers. It does make packing and unpacking simple. You can hang the opened valet bag right over the hangers in the closet, zip it up and you're ready to go.

Climate Variations

One might think traveling from one extreme weather condition to another would require more luggage. Depending upon the length of stay, the wardrobe space will vary more according to the person than according to the climate. When you travel from warm weather to cold, or vice versa, the answer is found in a layered wardrobe. Once you start thinking in terms of coordinated and compatible clothing you'll find that your mind is racing ahead toward all the possibilities each time you are about to make a new purchase. You can wear layers without the "layered look." For an extreme example, if you are leaving ice and snow enroute to balmy beaches, don't start out wearing a heavy winter coat and cumbersome fur-trimmed snow boots which will become an albatross about your neck in the land of sunshine. As an alternative, you might start out with a long-sleeved print blouse under a solid color, long-sleeved pullover sweater, over which you will wear a matching or color coordinated coat sweater. Assuming it is really freezing, opt for colored leotards under your slacks or skirt and an extra pair of woolen socks under soft vinyl, dark boots. A pretty, bright and lightweight poplin coat, warm and cozy gloves and a matching scarf or muffler will keep you cozy. Save some extra room in your carry-on to pack some of these garments as the temperature dictates. Upon your arrival the leotards, woolen socks, gloves and muffler can be rolled tightly and tucked away in a minimal amount of space. The blouse and pullover become separates you will enjoy when temperatures drop after the sun goes down. Also keep that coat sweater available for restaurants, theaters and other public areas where air conditioning may give you a chill. Hot tropical climates often tend also to short tropical showers so the poplin raincoat is well chosen.

Extended Trips

Are you one of the fortunate few who are looking forward to a four or even six-week trip? The thought of packing for it is almost staggering! Where to start? *Start* by thinking in terms of one week. That's right, *one* week. Pick up a pencil and write a list of the clothes you wore last week. Now, close your eyes and think back to the week before that. If possible, stretch way back and try to review a full month's clothing—

in general, the things you have worn over the past month. Notice the repeats? Everyone has their favorites that pop up very regularly, often weekly. Just for the record, most people wear about twenty percent of their clothing eighty percent of the time. Reversed, this means that eighty percent of the things in your closet you may wear about twenty percent of the time. With those percentages any of the twenty percent deserve to come along on the trip.

One final word about suitcases particularly on extended trips. *Never* pack any one case so large, or so heavy that you cannot lift and handle it yourself should that become imperative. At some time, it will probably be necessary for you to move your own things. Even on the fully escorted tours, there will be times when you must pick up and carry your own case. If you must pack that much, ship it to your destination.

LESS IS MORE

In my recently published book on time management, I suggest the reader print those words on a large sign. They are to guide her as she begins to discard (or at least remove to storage) unused articles which clutter up her home. The words "less is more" also apply to packing a suitcase. They force you to make decisions. Every mistake in packing results from a moment of indecision. Has this happened to you?

You open your closet door and reach for your favorite pantsuit. Great! It's your best color, looks crisp and fresh, and you know you'll enjoy wearing it on the trip. *"For sure, you'll take it! And next?"* You take a dress from the closet, look at it and think, "Well, maybe I will be needing this, if—"

Stop! The moment you hear yourself saying, *"Maybe—"* or *"If"* put it back in the closet. Pack only the *for sures.* Those two words are dynamite. *"For sure* I will take those comfortable shoes and my three-year-old sweater coat that wraps me in a cloak of comfort.

Packing becomes complicated when one considers *what* to pack. Reverse your thinking and ask what *not* to pack. Do not pack *"Ifs"* or *"Maybes"*; pack only the *for sures!* That is your control. Just as the mental image of the sarcastic face helps to put a heavy piece of luggage in the right perspective—the same works with clothing. Each article of clothing either works for you or against you, and if a garment has not earned its way into your case, the price is too high.

Actually, packing may be left till last provided the decisions concerning what to pack have been made in advance and it is simply a matter of placing your things in the suitcase. In fact, that is preferable. But if the decisions have not been made in advance, the pressure of packing at the last minute will cause you to take too much and all the wrong things. Don't be pressured—plan what you will take early—and give each garment a dress rehearsal to be certain it is right for the trip.

I can almost hear you saying, "What about the new things I just bought—or, what about the new things I want to buy?" You're right, you do need new things on a trip. They provide a natural high when they help you look your best. But select with care. This means special attention to color and comfort. Clothing must fit correctly to feel comfortable. A color that complements your complexion and is compatible with the rest of your travel wardrobe is a sure winner. Think about your favorites in the closet—your *for sure* clothes. They are comfortable and color coordinated—right? The first step in coordinating clothes for a trip is to choose two basic colors. Black and white is always striking—or you may prefer beige and brown—or rust and gold—whichever colors are best for you. Keep the basics to only two and build around them.

When you have removed the *for sure* garments and accessories from your closet or chest of drawers, place them on the bed or a rack so you can look at them as a distinctly separate "travel" wardrobe. Mix and match and see where you need a new blouse, an all-purpose wrap or other addition that will give extra versatility to your basics. I use index cards on which I write down every article of clothing and the accessories I will need for each outfit. In this way I can move the pieces around and often new ways of coordinating sets become apparent. This may sound like extra work but before you judge, give it a try. Oftentimes, one small purchase, or even adding a blouse you hadn't planned to take, will allow you to mix and match and create a whole different outfit. And, of course, the most important result is a well-organized suitcase.

Space Saver Secret

This may be hard to believe until you try it. The excitement of this packing message is a personal top secret that I'll share with you this very minute. Packing in nylon hose results in condensing a travel wardrobe into a minimum amount of space.

Take some of your nylon hose with runs and if you wear panty hose, just snip each hose off at the top of the leg. You now have two instant miniature packing tubes. Do *not* cut the toe off the hose. Now, take a long evening skirt that you are planning to take on your trip. Perhaps it is an accordion pleated or a gathered skirt and you have realized it will take up a good deal of room. You are going to be delighted to see the results when you follow my next instructions. Place the skirt on your bed and roll it lengthwise softly. This means from side to side and not from top to bottom. You now have a skirt, rolled. It will be given a covering to keep it from moving about in the case, and that cover is the nylon hose. It would be ever so much easier if I could demonstrate this next step to you as I have been doing all over the country as part of my suitcase packing demonstrations for American Airlines; however, read carefully and you will find it is very simple to do.

Pick up the nylon hose and with both hands roll the hose down to the toe, exactly as you do when preparing to put on a pair of nylons. The top of the garment will be placed in the toe of the hose. Hold the toe of the hose (that is now filled with the first couple inches of your skirt) keeping a firm grip with your left hand and with your right hand, pull the hose easily down and over the rest of the skirt. You now have a cushioned garment that is encased within a soft and light tube of nylon.

How about trying a few more items? The bulky sweater becomes a third of its size when contained in a nylon hose. Your lingerie is slipped easily into a hose; sleepwear, robes, swimwear and coverups. The longer dresses you may want to fold one time at the waist before starting the lengthwise roll to assure fitting into the stocking. With the exception of support hose, you will be surprised at the length your hose will stretch.

The benefits of this tube packing are recognized the moment you see how much space is saved. Also you have great control of the fabrics, like nylon, dacron and the slippery wash and wear items that tend to slip and slide so easily. This method keeps each garment contained and allows you to remove any one article without disturbing the other things. You will especially find packing soft-sided luggage, shoulder bags, and tote bags or, for that matter, any size or shape bag is easy when you use individual tubes of clothing. Many times, I demonstrate how an entire ten-day wardrobe can be placed in a shoulder tote bag when using this method. Seeing is really believing and because I cannot be there to show you how great this is, I encourage you to try a few pieces right now. Just roll lengthwise, slip a nylon over the garment and see how it works. Test it overnight and check in the morning to see how good your clothes look.

Before I conclude this section, I want to explain how I first started packing in this manner. During a European shopping trip, I purchased a number of prints that I planned to frame after returning home. The pictures were carefully rolled and a cardboard tube slipped over them. When I returned to the hotel room and started to pack my clothing, it occurred to me that every fold I made in a garment resulted in a crease. The principle of rolling prints, pictures, and maps is to prevent creases. Consequently, I adapted the same thought to packing and started to roll my clothing. The nylon hose was a natural tube that I had handy. That day seems a long time ago and I have shared this message with hundreds of delighted audiences. Hopefully, the information is clear and easily understood in this written explanation because I very much want you to realize the many benefits that tube packing can bring to your travels.

Dual Purpose Items

Each time you eliminate an item by finding one that will do double duty you are really saving yourself time and space—and money too. Here are some examples—

Often a beachwrap will double for a nightgown or a bathrobe.

Beach scuffs double as slippers in hot weather.

A travel tote bag can double for a beach bag or a shopping carry-all.

Huge scarves can work in many ways—as a shawl for cool evenings, a sarong over a swimsuit and as a great coverup for wrapping into fashionable turbans.

Most important of all, if you feel there is a certain article of clothing or an item you would like to have for a trip but it isn't essential that you have it immediately—wait and shop for it during your trip. Not only will it serve the purpose for which it was originally intended but it will also become a cherished memento of your trip. Particularly when you are limiting the possessions you carry along, it becomes even more important that they are meaningful. What fun if, each time you pack your hibiscus print swimsuit cover (which doubles as a housecoat), you are reminded of your first Hawaiian holiday.

Should you feel an urgency on my part to convince you to pack light—you are absolutely correct! The reasons are many but at the top of the list is that it is an important way to "be good to yourself." You will also be good to the friend or business associate meeting you. When they ask, "Where are your bags?" how delightful to be able to say—"this is it!" and to watch their surprised and admiring expressions. Traveling light is the mark of a real traveler.

*I look upon every day as lost in which
I do not make a new acquaintance.*
— Samuel Johnson

Four

DEPARTURE

One morning you awaken and a glorious feeling of anticipation haunts you. Your mind makes an attempt to focus— then suddenly—the message is clear. The day you have been looking forward to has arrived. This is the day of departure.

Take a few delicious minutes to daydream and anticipate your trip. Your usual routine of racing against time can be put aside and from this moment a new rhythm of relaxation and joy is going to be yours. The packing is finished and your checklist has eliminated any doubt that you might have overlooked anything. Your preplanning has given you a cushion of time in the event of any last minute emergency. The day begins with bright anticipation and will continue so, because your attitude is positive.

If you are traveling by car, plan your trip realistically so you don't arrive at your destination exhausted. If it is longer than you can drive and arrive in time to relax a bit before dinner, plan to stay overnight enroute, so you will arrive fresh and relaxed the following day. Check-in time is usually not before noon anyway. Remember, you are *not* engaged in an endurance contest—you are taking a holiday.

Should you be traveling by bus, train, ship or plane, you have most likely made advance arrangements with a friend to take you to the station, depot, dock or terminal. You may wish to take the opportunity while you are away to have your own car fully serviced and left in the mechanic's garage during your absence.

If you are taking a taxi, be sure to call early enough so there isn't a delay. Better to spend some extra time before departure at the terminal than at home, panic stricken that you will be late.

Park and Fly Lots

If you are leaving from your local airport and are not going to be gone for more than a week or so you may prefer to drive yourself. However, long-term parking rates are being raised higher and higher to discourage travelers from leaving their automobiles parked for any length of time in order to clear the area for short-term needs. As more airports are faced with this problem, "Park and Fly" lots are popping up miles from the terminal buildings. The concept is both essential and economical. Their courtesy car will take you and your luggage from the lot to the airline terminal, letting you out right in front of your check-in area. If you are planning to use their services, you may wish to call them and ask what their by day or by week charges are. Also inquire about how much additional time you should allow to get to the terminal. If you follow their advice you need not be concerned about missing the courtesy car that takes you to your airline. The service is frequent and dependable.

Of course, there are still some delightful small airports that seem warm and friendly to the first-time traveler. There is also a trend now toward using satellite airports in metropolitan areas to cut down on both ground and air traffic in the vicinity of the airport and in the interest of noise abatement. For example, many of the New York area flights depart from Newark and the San Francisco area flights depart from San Jose.

Please Notice

Whatever your choice of transportation, take the time necessary to look around as you enter a strange depot or terminal to orient yourself to its layout of ticket counters, baggage check, transportation in and out since if this is your point of departure, it will also most likely be your point of return. Be sure to take advantage of the facilities and conveniences available for your comfort.

For example, are you aware of the items available at most "gift shops" or "newsstands" found in depots and terminals? It is really amazing what a wide variety of really vital articles they carry and I am sure the inventory is based upon past requests. The selection may not be wide; but you will find everything from shower caps, to corn pads, and insect repellants to perfumes, in addition, of course, to the most forgotten item of all—toothbrushes.

It is in the best interest of everyone involved in the travel industry to make travel as convenient as possible, but as the number of people traveling increases the complexity of the terminals has also necessarily increased.

Usually above the check-in counter of most airline terminals, bus or train depots, you will find a large board with departure and arrival information posted as well as gate numbers and any schedule changes. If there is a discrepancy or if you have any questions, do not hesitate to verbally confirm the information with the agent on duty.

If you did not receive a schedule or timetable earlier, do ask for one at the counter and take a few minutes to study it. You may want to spend more time familiarizing yourself with it once you are on board your bus, train or plane. It is well worthwhile to have an idea of alternative schedules should an opportunity arise to take an exciting side trip or pursue another activity that would require a change of plans.

Tipping

According to legend, tipping originated in an eighteenth century English inn, when the innkeeper set out a little slotted box labeled—"To Insure Promptness." Guests dropped coins in the box if they wished speedy attention. Soon the acronym, TIP, and the custom spread around the globe.

Unfortunately, the original simple concept of tipping has turned into a complex problem for the traveler since it is difficult to know where and how to tip correctly. Today the norm for most services is approximately fifteen percent. Try this simple method to compute the tip. Move the decimal one place to the left to give you ten percent and then add half that amount again. Should you have a dinner bill for $20.00, move the decimal one place to the left to indicate ten percent or $2.00, plus half (five percent is $1.00), totals $3.00 or fifteen percent. When an odd amount is being figured, think in terms of the nearest dollar and work only in round figures— so much easier.

On an escorted tour check the small print to see if baggage transfer and gratuities are included. If they are, the tipping has been included in the price of the tour. However, when the same bus or limousine driver has been with a group for several days or weeks, he usually receives a collective reward.

A Friendly Bit of Advice

As far as food and drink are concerned, whatever you do, don't let go of your willpower when you are traveling. Particularly on cruises or on flights, do not indulge past a moderate limit, because the discomfort will not be worth it. A drink or two and the meal will suffice in most cases. Often, only a portion of the meal may appeal to you. Do not feel committed to eat everything because of a false sense of manners or because you have paid for it and therefore it seems only right to eat it all. Not so—the hours you may regret the overeating offset that philosophy. Instead, test your will-power a wee bit and it pays big dividends.

Keep in mind that your attitude and the atmosphere you create will determine how pleasant a holiday you will have. Should a delay, or even a cancellation occur try to think positively. If you find yourself getting anxious and uptight, stop and look at the situation objectively. Don't take yourself too seriously. Getting upset isn't going to improve things. Remember there are probably many others who are as inconvenienced as you with the delay or cancellation. Talk with them, share your concern for their needs. If you can't help them, often just listening will help. The result will be the pleasure of an unexpected new friendship and possibly an even better vacation.

Modern Motorcoach Travel

If you haven't ridden a bus in recent years you are in for a surprise. They have changed considerably to include comfortable, spacious seating with gigantic clean windows which provide an unrestricted panoramic view of the countryside. They are air-conditioned and equipped with lavatories for your comfort. The escorted modern motorcoach tours highlight geographical areas such as the Fall Foliage Adventure Tour through the New England states that attracts thousands of visitors annually. Each trip is carefully planned to overnight in the most interesting locations as well as allow sufficient time for sightseeing. In the same manner, on the other side of the continent, the Santa Fe Trail tour covers the great Southwest including the London Bridge at Lake Havasu, Tombstone, Phoenix, Tucson, Colorado Springs and Salt Lake City. Each area is covered with emphasis on points of interest from the East Coast to the West.

Aside from escorted tours, if you are planning a holiday at

a resort within driving distance and it is sufficiently self-contained so you won't need your car while you are there, do consider taking a bus. The well-known busline advertising, "Leave the driving to us," becomes very meaningful when you can sit back and relax in the comfort of a Scenicruiser, particularly if you are headed over mountainous terrains. You can avoid the strain and responsibility of driving with convenient schedules departing from East Coast cities for Catskill resorts and Atlantic Coast beaches; northern Californians have easy access to Tahoe's casinos and ski lodges and southern Californians to Las Vegas and Mexico.

A great bargain is available providing unlimited travel in America and Canada for the traveler who wants the freedom to plan an unhurried trip. The Greyhound Ameripass is available for seven or fifteen days or if you have more time, a great savings is available when you purchase a month or even two months' unlimited transportation. This could be an ideal vacation if you wish to spend time with friends and relatives in various locations. A cross-country trip can develop an appreciation for the great land that is America, her people, and their way of life.

Think a moment about the simple pleasures that we take for granted. The ability to walk, run, and move swiftly wherever we want to go is a gift denied the handicapped. The world can be a small place when imprisoned by limited mobility. Greyhound established its "Helping Hand" service in 1975, recognizing and removing many of the barriers to travel encountered by the handicapped. The service allows a handicapped person and companion to travel on a single ticket. The only requirements are that the pair travel together for the complete trip, and that the companion be capable of assisting the disabled person in boarding and exiting during the trip. Special brochures are available which explains this exceptional service in greater detail. I am personally eager to share this information with you and encourage anyone you might know who is handicapped to take a trip, arrange for a companion and enjoy the beauty and the pleasure of land travel.

My mother and her sister still speak with glowing memories of their Greyhound trip from the Midwest to San Francisco. They boarded the bus with a picnic basket filled with homebaked bread, sausages, cheese, date bars, cookies and fruit. They boarded the motorcoach in Des Moines and by Omaha everyone had shared their food, listened to their plans for the coming weeks and were caught up in the enthusiasm and excitement of the journey. When they stepped off the bus in San Francisco, I was introduced to a long line of their "friends" which further validates my point that it is indeed the people and not the places that live in our memories. In addition to food, the following will assure your comfort on a motorcoach or an auto trip of any distance.

- Dress comfortably. Bring a sweater and stocking slippers.
- Pack foods that keep well and include energy snacks.
- Wear sunglasses and pack a night shade for your eyes.
- When rest stops or meal hours allow, do stretch and move about.
- Take along a transistor radio with individual earplugs.
- A small tote bag should include basic grooming items so you may freshen up at rest stops.
- Wash and Dri packets are excellent, the prefolded and scented paper washcloths conveniently packaged in foil.
- Plastic bottles containing moisturizer, lotion, and cologne.
- Carry a trip diary and all important information, including emergency phone numbers, a list of your traveler's checks, address labels, picture postcards you buy along the way, and always stamps for mailing.
- A coin purse with ready change for phones, bathrooms, and tipping is welcome when you need it. Keep replenishing.
- Several small packets of Kleenex.

Train Travel

AMTRAK, the National Railroad Passenger Corporation is restoring America's skeletal passenger rail system. Traveling by train holds nostalgic memories and an aura of adventure and excitement for most people. In the United States, day coaches have comfortable two-abreast seating, with deluxe swivel arm chairs in first-class cars. Overnight trains have special sleeping cars with bedrooms, double slumbercoaches, and bedroom suites. Be sure to inquire about all the different types of accommodations and facilities available when booking your train to be sure you are not being pennywise and pound foolish when a savings of a few dollars might result in a less than comfortable trip.

If you seek total solitude with hours for quiet reflection and undisturbed privacy to be alone with your thoughts, a trip by rail is unequaled. As the train rushes along, the beauty of nature and land unmarked by highways, billboards and advertising, touches you with peaceful serenity. You will feel rested, refreshed and restored because you have given yourself time to unwind.

*Freelance writer Jay Freeland polled a group of AMTRAK executives, who would be presumed to know the system best, and emerged with the following as the *most scenic, regularly scheduled* train rides in the United States:

1. Through the High Sierra, between Reno and Sacramento, on the Chicago-originating *San Francisco Zephyr.*

2. Skirting the Pacific shore for 113 miles between Ventura and San Luis Obispo on the Los Angeles-Seattle *Coast Starlight.*

3. Crossing the Raton Pass (7,588 feet) on the Colorado-New Mexico state line riding on the Chicago-Los Angeles *Southwest Limited.*

4. Through Glacier National Park, 56 miles of soaring peaks with glaciers, on the Seattle-Chicago *Empire Builder.*

5. Following a trail blazed by Lewis and Clark, as the Chicago-Seattle *North Coast Hiawatha* twists through Montana's Homestake Pass.

6. For 142 miles, New York City to Albany-Rensselaer, running beside the mighty Hudson River on any of the *Empire Route Turboliners* or the *Lake Shore Limited.*

7. On the *Adirondack,* beside the Hudson, too; then alongside Lake Champlain on its daily daylight run between New York and Montreal.

8. Some of the East's most beautiful mountain scenery, through West Virginia, from the *Shenandoah,* linking Washington and Cincinnati.

9. The Great Horseshoe Curve, near Altoona, Pa., aboard the eastbound daylight *National Limited* or *Broadway Limited.*

10. A dramatic cityscape—Manhattan's towers, as seen gliding into the city, crossing Hell's Gate Bridge, aboard an *Amfleet* train from New England.

---

*Passenger service news, "The Official Railway Guide, June 1977

Train travel generally offers the opportunity to change into lounging garments and since long periods of sitting are typical, be sure to be comfortable. Avoid any restrictive clothing.

Also, although most passenger trains allow two pieces of carry-on baggage per passenger in addition to three pieces of checked luggage (not to exceed 150 pounds) do not take anything that you cannot comfortably carry yourself. Do not be misled to think that anywhere and everywhere on trains there is always someone to handle the bags. On many occasions it will be entirely up to you. Best to be prepared and travel light.

Traveling by train offers the advantage of departing from the center of town and means you will arrive at your destination in the town or city rather than having to arrange for miles of travel to your hotel. In most cases it is just a few minutes by taxi. So hail a cab—especially if it is after nightfall and treat yourself to getting to your hotel, settled, refreshed and carefree.

Ship Travel

If your cruise departs from the city where you live you will be one of the fortunate ones whose personal friends can attend your ship's bon voyage party. The festive aura that engulfs those about to start on a holiday cruise is infectious to all.

Cruises usually provide full service, leisure hours, superb cuisine and programmed activities both on board and at the ports of call. The first hours of your ship experience set the tone for the entire trip. Smile often. Allow your personality to sparkle. This is the perfect occasion to let your hidden extroverted personality surface—the one you keep dormant because of what "others" might think. Those "others" are nowhere around and this is the day to turn over a new leaf. Express yourself and you will find people eager to get to know you. The ability to look on the light side of things will cause others to seek you out and engage you to join in their plans on board and ashore.

When you book your cruise ask your travel agent for a chart of the dining room seating. Look at the size and placement of the tables and make a note of where you think you would like to be seated. Then, *on the day of departure,* to insure your being assigned a good table, arrange to speak with the head dining-room steward *early*. Ask his help with your table reservations. Explain that you have studied the chart and prefer a certain location. Ask that he include you with a large table of active people. The law of averages will be on your side when your choice of conversation is with many, as opposed to an assignment to a smaller table where it may be an effort to keep an interesting conversation going with two or three people. If there are two dinner hours, referred to on ship as "sittings," the first may be about 6:30. Do not book the first sitting! Families and senior travelers prefer the earlier hour and for you the first sitting means a shorter cocktail hour and ties you into an early breakfast. Far better to book the second sitting and linger over coffee and conversation, with the luxury of sleeping later in the morning.

With that detail settled, set out to see the deck steward about a deck chair. Select a "wind-free" spot—exposed to just the right amount of sun. Tall order—just ask the person who knows. I encourage you from the moment the trip starts to recognize every person as a potential ally. Treat every member of the staff, the manager, deck steward, and dining-room captain with caring diplomacy. You will be glad you did.

You may be stopping at several ports of call for shopping and sightseeing. You may choose to pace your activities by going ashore a few hours and then returning to enjoy the rest of the day in the ship's swimming pool or chatting with fellow passengers from the comfort of a deck chair. The social director will have a schedule of events, programs, parties, and even morning exercise planned for guests who wish to participate. The result is a party atmosphere that soon envelops the entire ship and all passengers glow with a feeling of belonging. Often one evening will be promoted as the most original costume, or passengers will be asked to dress as their favorite actress, book heroine, or political personality. Your travel agent may have an advance social schedule. Ask him if any costume parties are planned, and if so, slip a few items into your case that will give you more than a slight edge. From the time you are declared the winner, everyone on board will single you out as special.

A Word About Tipping on a Cruise.

It is accepted practice to tip once a week on cruises and, in general, think in terms of approximately five percent of your passage as an appropriate amount. It is customary to give tips in envelopes and with the recipient's name written on the outside. You will be given the names of crew members and it is in good taste to use the name of the cabin steward, the deck steward, the wine steward, the dining-room waiter, and any crew members who have extended service during your travel aboard ship. A good guide is about $1.50 per day per person and should you request special services such as the maitre d' arranging a party for you with hors d'oeuvres, glasses, mixes—a tip of $5 or $10 is expected. Remember that you never, *never* tip the purser or any of the ship's officers. Because tipping is an inevitable part of every trip, it is wise to preplan and budget for this expense so you will be prepared.

You have probably guessed by now that I feel cruising is a very relaxed and special way to travel. If space allowed, I would continue for chapters to share my reasons for encouraging everyone to take a cruise—at least one time. There is really nothing that can quite compare.

Airline Travel

During peak travel hours, the metropolitan airport may look like a nightmare of both vehicle and passenger traffic. If a relative or friend is taking you to the airport, it is wise to have them drop you and your bags at the curb on the departing flights' level. While you are checking in they can park the car and then perhaps join you for a cup of coffee or a cocktail before departure. If you are arriving by courtesy car or bus your driver will have asked what airline you are traveling on and will generally stop right outside the entrance to your ticket counter.

At larger airports, many airlines employ Sky Caps who are available to tag the bags, hand you the baggage claim checks and your luggage is checked right through to your destination. This is especially convenient if you are already ticketed and have made reservations since you can check the flight information posted behind the counter (often on closed circuit television) to learn from which gate your flight is scheduled to depart and then proceed directly to the gate for check-in, rather than having to wait in line at the ticket counter.

You may prefer to check in at the counter and check your bags with the counter agent since he will be able to answer any questions you may have concerning the flight. The counter agent will most likely staple the claim checks to the inside of your ticket envelope and write your gate number and time of flight departure on the outside. Whether you actually check in at the ticket counter in the terminal building or at the gate where you board your aircraft, you will be handed a boarding pass, and, for most transcontinental flights, given a seat assignment.

Federal regulations require all persons and carry-on bags (including your purse) pass through a metal detector before you may proceed to the boarding area. Simply place your belongings on the conveyor belt or lay them in front of the person on duty. Then wait your turn to walk through the doorframe. Your belongings will be returned to you on the other side of the security check.

Depending upon the hour of the day or evening, you may wish to have a cocktail if you have some extra time before your flight departs. Where is the perfect place to enjoy a drink in quiet elegance and in an atmosphere that allows the woman traveler to feel like a lady when ordering a cocktail? Where may she share conversation with others gathered together waiting for an airline departure? It is *not* the airport cocktail lounge. I asked hundreds of women their personal feelings about drinking or dining out alone while traveling. The majority agreed they felt awkward about going into any cocktail area unescorted or without a female friend.

The answer to both questions is membership in one or more of the clubs sponsored by major airlines, such as American Airlines' Admiral Club, the Trans-World Airlines' Ambassador Club or the Pan American Airways' Clipper Club. Most of the larger airlines have their own club and it is available for membership to those paying a yearly fee or purchasing a lifetime membership. While you are enjoying the luxurious refinement of the club, the hostess, who is in charge of the desk, will check on your ticket and provide your boarding pass. Additionally, she is in direct touch with the departure desk and will alert you in the event of a delay or change of departure gates. Any messages may be delivered to you and the convenience of many phones allows you to complete any last minute business or social calls.

Often the interesting person you share conversation with in the club offers suggestions of favorite restaurants, hotels, things to see and may even extend an invitation that you telephone friends or business associates of theirs in the city you are to visit. The trite phrase, "It's a small world," becomes surprisingly realistic when one starts to travel. I can think of no one single better investment for the woman traveler than that of membership in the club of her choice. Any time she is waiting at a major airport, the conveniences of the club are for her to use and to enjoy.

Once you are aboard the aircraft the flight attendant will help you get settled. Relax and enjoy your trip. Movies are shown on many of the transcontinental trips, and you will be offered several choices of entree, cocktails and soft drinks. In general, you will be entertained, fed, and watched.

Shirley Temple Black was asked what secrets she could share that helped her during the long air flights she was making regularly in her diplomatic role. Her comment was to make a regular practice of drinking lots of water in flight. How true. You will notice a loss of moisture in your skin, your face will appear much dryer and your hands need additional creams and lotions. Keep a small plastic bottle of lotion in your bag and use it frequently.

A word of support to anyone who has ever been shocked at the reflection staring back at them from the huge mirror in the lavatory. The lighting is "awful," and untrue! Do not let it disturb the glow you felt following the ice cold martini and the promising conversation with your attractive seat partner. Instead, turn the high glare to dim immediately. You can see adequately, those harsh shadows are removed and you feel a hundred percent better. The daylight filtering through the plane windows is natural lighting and flattering to the woman and is the way you appear to those in the cabin. Why something has not been done to create a more natural light in the lavatories, I do not know.

Incidentally, you are not alone if you find extra pounds seem to appear mysteriously during flight. You may notice swelling of your feet (your shoes refuse to go back on easily after you have slipped them off during the hours inflight). Especially uncomfortable are restrictive foundation garments. One airline reported the most common article turning up in their lost and found—ladies girdles! Take *that* as a measure of advice on selecting your travel wardrobe. I always suggest to women that it is smart to avoid waistbands altogether if possible. The elastic type is the exception and quite popular. Ideally, a one piece garment that glides over the body and is void of belts and bands proves a friend to wear enroute.

Watch for the relaxed time during the flight when you can speak with the flight attendants. They are professional travelers and their training provides a wealth of information. It is all yours for the asking and do ask! During my years as a stewardess I was always eager to share experiences but only when the passengers indicated a desire to talk. Once I was turned on to a conversation about sightseeing, restaurants, bargains, or clothes—it was difficult to remember I had duties to my other passengers. When you realize the flight crew has been trained in the art of assuring all passengers comfort, privacy and service—you will recognize this means they are sensitive to your quiet nature and interpret it to mean that you do not wish to be disturbed. Don't make the mistake of failing to use the hours enroute to further enrich the vacation you have planned. Anyone who feels shy about starting a conversation should think about the words of Benjamin Franklin:

"When you are good to others, you are best to yourself."

The simple act of being good, kind, and sincere to another will cause any feelings of shyness to disappear and allow your true self to surface. Direct the conversation toward the other person's interests. Ask about his trip. Find out if he or she has vacationed where you are going. The conversation rolls along easily when you are a good listener. Being a good listener is an acquired art that will assure your having continuing friends.

Upon arrival you exchange the comfort and security of the airplane for the impersonal atmosphere of an airport. Right at this moment, assume an attitude of control. Don't rush to wait!

In spite of my encouraging everyone to travel light, I am realist enough to know you have probably checked some bags. That is fine. I do hope you have taken only those you can carry, or purchased a case with wheels. Distances can seem forever if you are burdened with too heavy cases.

Let the others rush ahead of you to the baggage claim area. Take these minutes to visit your airline club in this airport. You will be warmly greeted by the hostess. Relax over a cocktail or cup of coffee and telephone your hotel to advise them you intend to check in shortly. Ask if you have any mail or phone calls.

I am going to share my very special secret that has proven invaluable to me. Before arriving in a city, especially during domestic travel, I send advance letters to my friends, business associates and potential clients. I give them my date of arrival, the name of the hotel where I will be staying, and ask them to jot down the best time I might phone them. For their convenience, I enclose a reply post card addressed to myself at the hotel with a large notation to the hotel mail desk.

PLEASE HOLD FOR GUEST ARRIVAL ON _____

The hotel has many guests and this will distinguish you from the masses and help them to remember you. The phone call you make from the airport is a second reminder. After you have shared conversation with the hostess, and any interesting persons in the club, it is time to claim your bags and hop the courtesy car, airport limousine, or cab to your place of lodging.

Should you have any question about transportation into the city, go directly to the ground transportation area, usually located on the lower level of the terminal building. Request information about the limo service into town or check to see if your hotel provides a courtesy car. Many hotels have direct telephones from the terminal to the hotel and they are usually found, clearly marked with the hotel name, on a wall adjacent to the baggage claim area. Simply pick up the receiver (there is no dial mechanism on this direct line) and the hotel operator will answer and send a courtesy car to pick you up.

Ground transportation may present a problem for the un-initiated traveler, but once you become accustomed to asking for information and then using airport trams, transfers, courtesy cars and whatever else is available, you will develop a self-assured attitude knowing that you are in control at all times. An airline sales representative summed it all up very well when he said, "The only foolish question is the one you didn't ask." Too many people are afraid they will appear stupid if they ask basic questions. Those are the very best kind to ask. Chances are in your favor that someone may know the answer and everyone enjoys being helpful. Make it a point to think in terms of *asking and sharing* and you will meet people easily. Perhaps the first times will seem awkward if you are shy or lack confidence; but this is an excellent time to practice the new assertive you. The trip can be an apprenticeship—by the time it's over the 'new you' that has developed may surprise even yourself.

To continually await the future is to overlook the obvious and miss the present. The hour of activity on a ship cruising to its destination could start a friendship that may completely change the direction of your holiday plans. If so, let it!! When traveling alone, the best plans can be thrown to the winds if you decide the alternative is more attractive than the original. The purpose of a holiday is to relax, to enjoy, and—to live!

Realization is indeed
Greater than Anticipation

—Goldfein

Five

ARRIVAL

When you reach your hotel, leave your bags at the bell captain's desk. A smile and a friendly greeting will indicate you are pleased to be a guest. Place your written confirmation and one of your business cards on the front desk and in a firm and friendly voice, tell the desk clerk your name and that you wish to check in. State your name clearly. This is important wherever you are staying. Continue to repeat your name to any member of the hotel staff with whom you are speaking. In addition to receiving the best possible service during your current stay, you will find good hotel people tend to register a guest's name and face in their mind and, incredible as it may seem, will recognize you when you return.

Be certain also that the hotel switchboard operator understands that you are registered, how to pronounce your name and that it is spelled correctly. A simple phone call soon after you are settled in the room will assure you of this. It takes only a moment to pick up the phone and ask the hotel operator if she has any messages for you. She will check and if the records are in order, her response will tell you if your room registration is correct. The number of times people seem to be misplaced in hotels seems unforgiveable. To prevent this, and possibly missing an important business call or a social invitation, take the precaution of checking to see if they do indeed know you are there. Another helpful hint is to explain you are expecting several important calls (even if you don't know a soul) and this will flag your name and make an impression on the mind of the operator.

I must restate the importance of a *written* confirmation of your reservation because sometimes a hotel will overbook and those without confirmations in writing are given a fast shuffle. Don't let it happen to you. Let the staff know that you expect your room to be available and stand firm if there seems to be any confusion. Silence, throughout any lengthy explanation on the part of a clerk or an assistant, is your best asset. When they finish speaking, tell them firmly and clearly that you want to speak with the manager. Rooms appear like magic when your control is felt and emotions are kept in check.

After you have registered, follow the bellman to your room and ask him to and show you how to operate the air conditioning, the television set and anything else in the room that may need an explanation. It is convenient to have all units working well immediately rather than to have a delay in service. Tip generously because the same person may be at your service several times during the following days. Treat the staff with the respect you would show a host and hostess. The comfort you enjoy depends upon the service they provide during your stay. It is up to you to enjoy every luxurious moment to the fullest and do show your appreciation to all those who contribute in making your stay pleasant.

Following a long trip, the body needs time to unwind and to recharge. Take this opportunity to be good to yourself. Do not rush out to see the world until you have rested. Draw a relaxing bubble bath, turn on the radio to a soothing melody, and release any thoughts from your mind that re-

quire concentration. Read something light or simply daydream while the warm bath soothes your mind and relaxes
your muscles. Very often a nap will seem like a good idea following the laziness of the bath. Your mental state will have
slowed down and because the holiday promises to be perfect,
it becomes apparent that care of oneself is the first step
toward having a great time. The world will wait— there is
always tomorrow.

Look and See

A new resort, city, town, or country can offer excitement
and intrigue. You may have in mind the things you want to
see as a result of your advance planning, but an important
first step in feeling comfortable in new surroundings is to
pick up a map of the area and orient yourself. Maps of the
city may usually be obtained in the lobby. If a city tour is
available, do try to take it. It will provide you with an
understanding of the local geography, and landmarks and
points of interest will become reference points. The historical
monuments, new buildings, schools, churches, and most interesting highlights will be included in an hour or two. I urge
you to take this tour early. It will allow you to be more selective with the rest of your time.

For example, when you return from the tour pick up the
local brochures and magazines that are provided in the hotel
lobby for visitors. Select a comfortable spot, perhaps with a
cup of coffee or glass of wine, and start reading about the
things you have just seen. Everything will be clearer and you
will recognize the general location of the places mentioned in
the brochures and have some idea of the distance and direction they are from your hotel. Clip the things you want into
your trip diary. If public transportation is convenient, don't
miss the double bonus this provides the traveler. You can be
kind to your budget and it will give you the opportunity to
meet people. To feel the pulse and rhythm of the country,

hop on a bus or take a subway. Just ask the bus driver what you need to know. Subway stations have clearly marked maps and the routes are easy to understand. Should you have questions, ask the person selling tokens, which you will need to board the subway or other underground system.

Should you take a taxi, do not indicate to the driver you are totally unfamiliar with the area or you may find out too late the driver has taken you for a *ride*. It is unfair to be taken on a circuitous route because you are a stranger, but it does happen and your innocence can cause a dent in your budget. It may be wiser to assume an air of confidence, state the address and say nothing more. Silence is golden and works in your behalf—the driver will take you directly to your address.

In fairness to drivers the world over, let me qualify the above with a true story and simply caution you to use your own best judgment about when to talk and when to remain silent. The driver in this case operated a thirty-passenger sightseeing bus on a daily tour of one of Hawaii's beautiful outer islands. The bus was equipped with a loud speaker and the native driver kept up a delightful chatter as he herded his happy throng through sugarcane fields and Buddhist temples. Between stops he pointed out the fantastic flora and fauna, punctuating his travelog with endearing anecdotes about members of Hawaii's royal families and other amusing stories. As the bus arrived back at the hotel every member of the group was feeling disappointed that all this fun was about to come to an end. Then one member of the group asked the driver if he could recommend some evening entertainment on the island.

True to character, the driver rose to the occasion and urged anyone interested in seeing a truly exceptional and authentic show to visit the lounge of one of the nearby hotels that evening. He further suggested that they come early in order to get good seats since the show was quite popular locally.

As you can imagine, the entire group lined the floor show area and were still talking about their delightful tour as they eagerly awaited the entertainment. Imagine their surprise when the Polynesian group (of which their driver was leader, head vocalist and father of several of the other members) appeared resplendent in matching outfits strumming Hawaiian guitars. The floor show proved to be everything he had promised and featured a group of beautiful native hula and Tahitian dancers (led by his lovely wife, of course). The entire group stayed until closing time.

This is the sort of experience that often happens in travel and as a result people easily become acquainted. I'm sure part of the reason is that, just like the truly exceptional travel agent mentioned earlier, persons who make their livelihood in the tourist industry tend to be extroverted and interesting. Perhaps travel attracts exciting people—or maybe it is the fact that travel is exciting that it attracts interesting people.

I encourage you to take part in a planned tour during your initial exploration. However, be alert to the moment you begin to feel comfortable with the area and select a charming local restaurant for your luncheon—alone. Speak with the proprietor and share your eagerness to learn about the region, about the people and their lives. Ask how long he has lived in the area and how long has the restaurant been there. Offer genuine compliments and be a good listener. The combination is dynamite. This is a brand new world and you can be anything and anyone you like. Become the new "you" that spells excitement and fun.

"Let a man make varied friends and he will lead a thousand and one lives."
            —Chinese Proverb

Six

ENJOY!

My purpose in sharing my travel experiences and providing direction is to help you avoid some of the usual disappointments and at the same time convert everyone within my reach into an enthusiastic traveler. We have discussed the decision to travel by carefully weighing the priorities to be considered. Following the decision of the "Why" and the "How, When and Where," you were encouraged to do the planning that is essential to a smooth and a simple trip. Complications result from the confusion of not having a plan. Let us assume you have planned well; the weeks and months of homework are about to pay you deserved dividends. Your holiday has begun to take shape because of the earlier city tour.

Now you are rested, refreshed and ready to enjoy both the place and its people. You may feel like contacting someone. This is the time to telephone the friend of a friend or the social organization or business contact. Pick up the phone, identify yourself, and ask her or him to join you for coffee or an afternoon cup of tea. This allows each of you a convenient exit if you find that the extent of your interest can be concluded over a cup of coffee. However, oftentimes that initial meeting will advance to a productive day of introductions to a new city and a great day to remember.

Should you find a phone call is met with hesitation or excuses, ask only an additional question or two—perhaps they will suggest a visit to a part of the city that is special to them but not included in the usual commercial tours. This type of conclusion to the conversation allows them to feel they have provided help and relieves them of any guilt for not meeting with you personally. You may wish to call several contacts, or, stimulated by the suggestion of a charming luncheon place, plan your day to include a leisurely luncheon and sightseeing.

I especially enjoy Frances Koltun's remark in her excellent book *The Intelligent Woman Traveler* written in 1967 (Simon and Schuster): "The secret of a good itinerary is counterpoint—the play of city sightseeing against country motoring, or a museum morning with a beach afternoon, of a string of capitals with a lake resort."

We encouraged you earlier to plan a schedule directed to your individual interests. You may wish to forego the long hours of visiting museums and art collections and indulge yourself with the feminine pastime of shopping. If so—do it! There is no one around to tell you that reviewing historical highlights must be your cup of tea. Remember—no one knows you as well as you do. Do not act as though a trip is an endurance test. A half day tour of Mexico City, for example, is far wiser than a full day that might overwhelm a first time visitor and prove exhausting. The change in altitude, climate and the food require time for the body to adjust and you need to be aware of this when you travel. Keep it loose and you'll have much more fun. If you prefer to eat your way around the world vs. strolling through churches and cathedrals—it is your choice to do so. I am reminded of an article

I enjoyed recently that described the Traveler versus the Tourist.

Definition of the Tourist: One who is passive and goes to the Louvre because it is the thing to do; dines at a top restaurant because Guide Michelin gives it a three-star honor; does everything because others say to do so. The result is too oftentimes boredom. Unable to quite recognize the reason, it is not until the tourist becomes a traveler that full happiness of travel is realized.

Definition of the Traveler: One who is active, curious and enthusiastic. One who is eager to see new places, explore foreign lands and enjoy the search. A traveler is aware of priorities and is continually alert to simple pleasures and personal comforts.

Perhaps British actor Robert Morley's definition says it best: "Remember, a tourist accepts, a traveler selects."

The Traveler Selects—morning coffee where the locals meet. How? This example may not be for everyone; however, if it appeals to you, give it a try. Pick up some newspapers and sling your camera over your shoulder; grab a shorthand pad, an official looking book or two and dress the role of a reporter on assignment. Head directly for the crowded coffee house and sit quietly for a few minutes and survey the scene. As the waiter returns to ask if you would like more coffee, explain you would like to ask him a few questions about the city. As you are talking with him, allow your voice to carry as you tell about the article you are writing and ask if he could suggest some local highlights and places of interest. More than one person may offer their ideas. Take notes as they talk. Playing the role of a reporter or writer gives an air of confidence and truly serves a good purpose. The suggestions you hear from the local residents will be more valuable than those of the guidebooks and local tourist bureau. For instance, think about the times you have suggested restaurants, places to see, things to do in your home city to those who are new in town. The chances are that your own favorites are small and intimate places that are special because they carefully guard their uniqueness and refrain from publicity. The very same applies when you are the visitor.

—and night cometh—

These are but a few remarks that I heard during my interviews with those who have traveled alone. The problem is dining and drinking alone in the evening.

> "Everything is fine during the day; however, night and the problem of eating and having a drink somewhere is a constant concern."
> "Only a self-reliant woman or man can travel alone happily—nighttime brings loneliness and spoils the fun of the day."
> "I would take a trip tomorrow, if only I didn't have to face the evening meals alone—and I simply detest tour groups!"
> "My vacations are glorious, during the day. The big problem has always been eating and drinking after dark."

Are you surprised? I was not because a woman does frequently feel embarrassed to enter a bar or a dining room alone. Should you feel the same anxiety, I have listed a number of excellent alternatives.

Prior to making reservations in large hotels, do ask your travel agent to check and see if they have a social hostess. Oftentimes, this is an immediate opening for introductions. She is employed for the purpose of arranging special cocktail

Enjoy!

and dinner parties to help guests become acquainted and, in general, blend into a happy and comfortable group.

If you are planning to stay in a certain hotel for a number of days, make a practice of dropping by for a late afternoon cocktail and share conversation with the bartender. You will not feel awkward at that hour and the alert individual tending bar will remember to introduce you to other guests of the hotel when you drop by during the usual predinner cocktail hour.

If you are staying in an area for many days, select a favorite little bistro in the neighborhood and drop by several afternoons for a cup of tea or a drink. When you mention that you plan to return for dinner in a few hours, the proprietor will be expecting you. The atmosphere will be warm and you will be sincerely welcomed. Remember this: The custom of seeking out a new restaurant every evening is a fallacy and running from here to there, testing and sampling, results in a culinary contest. Instead, find a favorite that suits your taste and return often to savor the friendship as well as the food.

A Nightclub Tour is available in almost every major city. It is a package designed especially for the lone traveler but will include couples, singles and families. One prepaid ticket will include cocktails at several top clubs and dinner at one of them before moving along to still another for a show and two drinks. The party ends well after midnight in most cases. I do think the price is well worth it for the places and shows you see. You may ask at the hotel tour desk or bell captain's desk for information on how you might book a reservation on the evening tour.

Should you be traveling in the Far East, it is quite acceptable to hire a full-time guide. The guide will take you sightseeing and to restaurants and the theater. You will pay a modest sum for this service.

Another help in easing the dining problem is to be alert during the day to possible desirable dinner partners. Almost always a single woman finds another equally single woman or man on the tennis courts, around the swimming pool or perhaps on a tour. It may seem awkward to you at first; however, it does become easier with practice.

Assume you are waiting in line for the tour bus to pick the group up and a young woman is standing next to you and looking at a city map. An easy opener is to ask if she has been on the half-day city tour. Because you have completed that tour, you can share the highlights and the conversation will start rolling freely. Ask the type of question that encourages an explanation. A straight yes or no builds an awkward silence and it takes skill in turning a communication with another into a comfortable patter. You must be careful not to seem too personal and yet avoid seeming distant. You may be eager to know the traveler better; however you are plagued by old memory tapes of caution which, in many cases, simply reflects a lack of confidence. Stop thinking about what other people might think and start to think about what you think. Would you really like to know that person better? They may be equally as eager to know you and the result will be a vacation filled with warm memories of people—rather than places.

When looking for alternatives, do program a few evenings to include local lectures, concerts, small theater productions, and church social activities. A quick check of the local paper will give you the information.

As a final word on the subject, don't underestimate the pleasure of your own company. Think about who you know better and how rare it is in your usual work week to enjoy pure privacy. Perhaps planning at least one evening every week to enjoy the luxury of room service and relax with a good book or have an early dinner and lights out would be an excellent habit to start. The practice can do wonders to recharge the batteries that too often start to wear down without your even being aware it is happening. In summary:

"No one can give you better advice than yourself."

—Cicero

Everything you decide upon and do during your special vacation is yours to direct and control. Keep this in mind when the days of your holiday are slipping by ever so quickly. Give yourself some good advice by listening closely to your own drum beat.

Let's consider some ideas or interests you may want to include on your holiday. The first is one you'll recognize:

Shopping

A travel agent friend has a favorite cartoon framed and enjoys the smiles it brings his clients. It shows a woman talking with the travel agent and the caption states:

"Don't tell me what there is to see!
Tell me what I can buy."

Most women like to shop and those who enjoy the "hunt" will find their hours of diligent shopping will surely uncover bargains and treasures. There is an added bonus if you are this type of shopper. Time spent in the small shops speaking with the proprietors, others who are shopping, and the local residents in the shop, will tell you more about a country than the monuments and churches. You learn how people furnish their homes, the clothing they wear, the food they eat and countless other human touches that are revealing.

Cooking Classes

Have you ever spent a portion of your holiday taking cooking lessons? Consider this if you would like to meet interesting people who share your interest. Make arrangements to enroll for the time you have available. For instance, a local newspaper may have a series of classes for every morning and you may decide that sounds great. Take only three out of six if this is more appealing. The fact one often eats the foods prepared will mean a saving on lunches with the added bonus of others to share the meal. Classes are frequently available in foreign countries as well as the United States. Ask your travel agent for information long before you actually arrive in the country. This will allow you to make a selection of dates and work your itinerary around the hours. Full tours devoted to the culinary arts are becoming popular and you might wish to consider one of these.

I heartily applaud anyone who picks up on self-improvement or instruction that is available. Balancing a totally carefree vacation with a few structured plans will result in inner satisfaction. The old puritan work ethic is not easily thrown aside and our beneath-the-surface emotions are sometimes hard to interpret. Handle this uneasiness with productive satisfaction by balancing a touch of learning with the freedom of unstructured time.

Participate in classes in yoga, dancing, meditation, quilt making or any subject you find interesting. The list is endless and if you have extended time in any one location, you will begin to feel like a resident. Community centers, the local YWCA, and churches are sources of classes that you might be interested in.

Maintenance Time

The term maintenance was suggested by a lovely woman of many years, who kept her age a secret and sparkled with a great zest for life. She was on a panel of experts during a convention I attended last year. A number of admirers complimented her following the program and in answer to their inquiries on how to retain one's appearance, she answered,

"It's all in maintenance, my dears. The years will treat one kindly only if one treats them with respect. It is a law of life that when growth ceases, decline begins. Thus, it is the duty and the goal of every person to continue growing both in thoughts and in ways to compensate for the aging."

When pressed to be specific, she spoke first about *attitude* and, second, the importance of taking *time* to protect and to preserve oneself.

Her explanation glided beautifully into the subject of the conference: Personal time management and how to achieve individual effective use of one's time.

Because the subject of time has been forever fascinating to me, I have recently put into book form a step-by-step guide that helps to direct a woman toward the goal of "Time for Oneself." The book, referred to earlier is titled *Everywoman's Guide to Time Management.* The first homework assignment is:

Take a hour of time for yourself each and every day. Use this time to refresh and recharge your mental and physical self. Use it to enjoy a warm and relaxing bath or a quiet time for reading, listening to music, or simply daydreaming. The hour works wonders and everyone owes at least that much to themselves.

When on a holiday, maintenance requires not overscheduling your day. Away from the comfort of your own bed, compensate by sleeping an extra hour or two many mornings. Forego a morning climb to the pyramids and climb instead onto a chaise longue or a massage table. Simple relaxation may be more pleasurable.

Visit a recommended beauty salon and have a facial as well as a shampoo. Many times women develop a loyalty to their hometown hairdresser and sacrifice an experience that might prove exciting. A brand new hairstyle can give you a lift and the feeling of confidence will make a good vacation even better.

Think of the times you look your best. Could it be that the

glow and sparkle of a few hours spent in maintenance time can assure you regularly looking your best? Of course it can, and today is not too soon to take time for yourself and profit by the results.

". . . The Louvre?
Why, that's where Mona Lisa lives!"
— Dean Goldfein

Seven

TRAVELING WITH CHILDREN

My youngest child voiced the above observation to a friend as they talked about his visit to Paris, and it confirms the very reason I am eager to share traveling with my family. In addition, the following statements will share more of my feelings about the reactions I have witnessed as a result of travel experiences

Travel is an educational experience for the young, the memories of which are carried into their adult lives.

To be touched by the sight of poverty and to learn respect for the pride of those less fortunate teaches compassion.

To taste foods that are different and to recognize the foreign languages and complex currency, creates awareness.

To thrill with the hope of returning to a place, to a country that helped expand one's horizon, encourages growth.

As I reflect upon the ages of my youngsters today, I recall how different travel was when they were very young. Because they are now ten, fourteen and fifteen, I am more alert to the needs and interests of older children. However, the memories of past vacations are still vivid.

If you have children, the first thing to consider when planning a trip is, "Would I prefer to take this holiday with the children or without them?" Allow yourself an objective and totally honest answer. Once the decision is made, the plans can be focused toward taking the youngsters or arranging for their home care.

For those who decide it is a good idea to take the children along, let's consider the early planning that must be considered in the same way we reviewed your preplanning schedule.

Involve your youngster in planning the trip.

Interest him or her in background reading and collecting maps, brochures, and literature to study.

Visit your children's doctor and be assured all vaccinations are complete many weeks before your trip.

Passports are needed for every person traveling outside of the country. If the child is under sixteen they may be included on either parent's passport at no extra charge. Note: I have found this useful in that you need only watch the safekeeping of one passport instead of four when traveling with the three children.

Write to the places you plan to visit and ask for a list of children's activities. In the States, the visitor and tourist bureaus have this information. Prepare a trip diary for the youngsters and have them add to it regularly during the trip.

Pack a first-aid kit containing bandaids, children's aspirin, antiseptic ointment, thermometer, suppositories, Kaopectate, a small scissors, tweezers, surgical tape, bandages, and include a small flashlight, some Wash 'n Dries, and a plastic bag containing a washcloth and soap.

Select a case that is right for your child and impress on him or her the responsibility of keeping and carrying it. It is essential that this habit be learned early if you are to enjoy the trip.

The trick to packing a youngster's clothing (before the teenage years) is to color coordinate them. It will result in many changes from a few good basics in solid colors. For example: two pairs of blue jeans and a couple pair of cords in a light blue will dictate shirts, one good wool sweater and a soft jacket in colors that coordinate with blue. This works as well using beige cords and a couple of dark brown pants. Remember that plaids, stripes and assorted colors are all losers on any trip because they must stand alone to look good. It is much easier for both the child and mother if a dozen solid white and solid blue knit shirts are packed. Laundry becomes simple, decisions are reduced to a minimum, and it is easier for the child to dress when everything matches. In truth, it is the parent who feels happier when the youngster looks coordinated. This method has worked for me both at home and away. Think about it—two basic colors and use solid knit shirts or sweaters for both boys and girls. The look is classic and everything can be dropped into the same laundry load.

Let your children wear favorite and comfortable clothing while traveling since coping with strange places is an adjustment that is less stressful when they feel the security of familiar things. Never buy a new pair of shoes for them just before a trip—plan ahead a few weeks and let them break them in before going. Don't overlook beach sandals if you plan to be near the water. Many times pool rules require bathing caps. To buy them there will result in an expensive purchase at the resort's boutique and sizes are often limited. Be prepared with earplugs, eyedrops, and any medications that might be necessary if your youngster has problems after swimming.

From one mother to another, anytime I take my children on a trip their sweaters, coats, and several shirts and blouses have their name tags sewn on the inside collar. In the case of an accident, the name is known to the authorities and, in the case of a very small child, a public announcement can be made for the parents in a department store when the identification is on a garment the child is wearing.

It is wise to place the name of your hotel (stationery or the return address of an envelope is easy to tear off) in your child's pocket or purse. When they do not have a pocket or purse I have each of the children put paper money of the country we are visiting and the name and address of the hotel inside their shoe. This is for a taxi return to the hotel if they should somehow become separated from me. Oftentimes one bill and one slip of paper is sufficient. With this precaution, you will feel more comfortable riding the public transportation, like the Metro of Paris, the subways around London and the glorious double decker buses. If the child does become separated from you, the anxious moments are quickly relieved when you find he or she has returned to the hotel in about the same amount of time it has taken you to get back. Children are very resourceful; however, a foreign city can be a maze for an adult and a traumatic experience for a youngster who does not have this plan in "his shoe." Make a game of it, as we have, and I think you will find it works beautifully—sure does for us.

We have talked about the planning and the packing. Let us get on with getting there. Think objectively about the ages of the children. Any type of transportation is restrictive so the younger the child the faster you should get to your destination. Plane travel is an absolute luxury. A bassinette may be arranged for the comfort of your baby on the aircraft by checking early with the airline and asking if the service is available. The seats aft of the first cabin must be reserved early and the bassinette is designed to attach to the bulkhead directly in front of your seats. If you are traveling with a toddler, the airport strollers that are now available in many terminals will be helpful. As you arrive at the gate early, ask the agent if you may preboard with your children. Many carriers are also providing hamburger and milkshake meals upon early reservation. The food service, movies, games and naps will result in thousands of miles traveled in comfort. Don't be premature in your decision against air travel because of cost. Look into the variety of plans available and consult your travel agent early to learn about plan-ahead fares, family travel, and the excellent "fly and drive" packages that provide a car and hotel arrangements all wrapped up in one convenient plan to suit your needs. When you are weighing which way to go, consider the number of hours invested in travel time and add the food and lodging costs for the same number of miles when using auto or ground transportation from your home to the place you are going.

Whatever your choice of transportation, planning for comfort enroute is first priority. Pack a carry-on case with small travel games and a few good books. Don't overlook one for yourself. Additionally, any carry-on case should be supplied with overnight items in the event your luggage does not arrive at your destination when you do. Cases can be misplaced. You can always be sure you have the necessary items when carrying them, and include any medications or prescriptions your children may need. If your youngsters wear glasses or contact lenses, a second pair is very important. Do a checklist countdown before leaving home and chances are in your favor that few things will be forgotten.

We are talking about transportation and because I have just returned from a trip through Italy, I must alert you about the summer travel by train in Europe. Never attempt to save money by booking a second-class reservation. The

American way of life has caused us to expect comfort, convenience and service. Vacation time is not pleasurable when these things are missing. Budget in other areas so that you can book first class, reserved seats on the European trains. We have regularly found it is delightful to plan a picnic on board. Purchase favorite foods before you take the train and you will have time to thoroughly enjoy the meal while traveling and it helps to pass some of the hours. The same plan for eating a meal enroute can be used when going by bus; however, the seating is more restrictive and often the bus route plans regular meal stops that are welcomed.

Let us move along and consider the ages of children and how an itinerary must vary to assure everyone's happiness. Until your child is about ten, comfort is going to have to count more than charm. Also, a daily routine that is close to the one the child enjoys at home is wise. Lazy resort life with American conveniences is best when the children are young. Never attempt an itinerary that exceeds the capacity of the child to adjust comfortably. As your children grow, they do become more flexible. The ability to take care of themselves builds confidence and allows the parents to relinquish control. This can be an enormous relief and I am personally pleased to have my children very self-sufficient as a result of travel which builds personal responsibility and self-confidence.

Accommodations: Advance reservations will prove important after a long flight and late arrival. Arrange for the children to have a room of their own if they are old enough. In the case of young children, an extra cot may be put in the room, and with advance notice, many hotels and motels can provide cribs if necessary. When traveling in the States, a good motel is convenient for a family instead of a highrise hotel. The cost will be less and often a pool, play area, ice machines, soft beverages, and even laundry facilities are available. Driving directly to the door is of help; hotel lobbies and corridors are really not the place for children to play or to be made to act as adults and walk and speak quietly. Vacation time is an occasion for fun and for great memories. Keep all of this in mind when arranging for your accommodations.

Food: A small kitchen, or perhaps just a refrigerator can be a great savings of money and sleep. Shopping the day you arrive for breakfast favorites will give you the luxury of relaxing late in the morning. Light snacks, even food for dinner, can be taken to the room for a welcome break instead of eating meals out all of the time. When you plan to eat in a restaurant, it is quite permissible to ask to see the menu *before* everyone is seated, drinking the water, putting down the napkins and it is too late to decide the meal is sure to blow your budget for a couple of days. An occasional expensive meal is given very special attention when it is treated with the respect it deserves. By balancing the cost of food with the grocery shopping, occasional picnics, a number of short order lunches and good, family restaurants—this plan should work well.

During some of the meal times, take the opportunity to hear suggestions from all members of the family about the plans for the next day. Too often, a lack of communication will result in disagreements because the children are having to follow along with everything the parents plan. To hear the children's thoughts will turn up some exciting ideas that parents overlook, and by listening, the trip goes much better. Always check on the local activities in the newspaper, special events calendar, hotel brochures, tourist information center or the visitor's bureau. Treat every city as though you were planning to spend some time—maybe even live there one day. With that objective in mind, you view a place differently and stop being a tourist and more a traveler.

Before we conclude the information about traveling with children, I want to explain the importance of arranging for some time alone, or if traveling with your husband, just the two of you sharing an evening or an occasional day out alone. Too much togetherness is unreal because it is not repetitive of what one has at home. The routine of school, work, and activities that separate the family allow a comfortable balance. On a family vacation, be alert to seek that balance by planning cushions of time that will be welcome to everyone.

For the very young, call a babysitter. In the United States, many hotels will provide a list of competent and reliable sitters. Agencies listed in the yellow pages are another source and, of course, any personal friends or relatives are a first choice if they are willing and available. In Europe, the concierge or hall porter at your hotel has a list of reliable sitters. Do avail yourself of this convenience.

When your children are a little older, the decision to leave them at the hotel or motel with a hamburger and milkshake in the room may be fine. The age of the child and where you are staying will determine if you want to call in a sitter. After the child is past ten and especially if older brothers or sisters are along, the evenings can be quite comfortable without worry or concern while mother and dad have a night on the town. One of the delightful bonus treats for a vacation overseas is the opportunity an American family has of enjoying the best of all worlds. If you have fairly self-reliant teenagers, consider allowing them the experience of a foreign summer camp. The fees are low and the style is American. For more information write to the Swiss National Tourist Office, 608 Fifth Avenue, New York, New York 10020. Ask about their special educational program and they will advise you about schools, camps, holiday courses and children's homes.

On this happy note, we will conclude the chapter and encourage your planning a family holiday that is filled with relaxation, rest and free of any routine. Have fun!!

"When in Rome do as the Romans do"
—by St. Ambrose giving a piece of advice
to St. Augustine about church customs.

Eight

INTERNATIONAL TRAVEL

Consider a trip abroad as an investment in your future. It will pay generous dividends for years to come. Should this be your first trip, I envy you. The general background you absorb on a holiday abroad will insure your wishing to return and explore specific places at another time. Your mind will race back to relive events and pleasant moments that you spent in Paris, walking the paths of history in Rome, marveling at the splendor of the Swiss Alps and recalling the kindness of the hostess at the guest home where you stayed outside of Lucerne. The joy of savoring those memories is the special bonus one receives following any glorious adventure in travel.

Read on to learn some of the answers you may have to questions about vacationing in foreign countries. Excellent books are available with specific and detailed information on travel to many places and your travel agent can suggest some when you are planning your trip. This chapter, as the book was intended, will give you general guidelines and my purpose is to excite your enthusiasm to travel and to start planning immediately.

To Tour Or Not To Tour

Volumes have been written on the pros and cons of this statement and it is really answered only by the individual who is planning the trip. Here are some guidelines that may help.

For the first-time traveler, a tour plan eliminates the problem of being alone and you see a great deal in a short time. Tours are economical because operators are able to offer group rates. The hotel space is reserved in large blocks of rooms and often an independent traveler during the busy season is unable to find reasonable hotel accommodations.

A disadvantage to the tour schedule is having to move along when you might wish to stay longer. Depending on the tour members, you may find personality clashes, and spending several weeks with the same group of people can be a test of patience. The exception is when a group shares the same interest.

For example, special tours are designed for bridge enthusiasts, opera aficionados, garden clubs, photography tours and other special interest groups. Gourmets love the popular cooking classes that include a week living in the area and enjoying the instruction led by a famous chef.

The opportunities are limitless. If a special tour appeals to you, do investigate before your trip. With a professional and understanding travel agent, you will put together an ideal package. A first step is to answer the why, how, when, and the where questions. Make an appointment and have a list of questions ready. Sit quietly and listen to the questions the travel agent asks and recognize that the clue to an exceptional agent will be the one who cares about your comforts and the type of accommodation and vacation that will be right for you. The agent may ask about your special interests, if you enjoy sports, art, music or have any particular hobbies. This information will give the agent a good sense of direction for the planning of the trip. Your questions will indicate you have completed some early decisions on the cost and the comfort that you want. Together, the excitement starts to build and you will enjoy the anticipation that builds as you move toward the day of departure.

Tipping Abroad

As you are comfortable tipping in the United States for services well given, the same should apply in other countries when you feel promptness has provided you comfort. The original definition "to insure promptness" is an excellent guideline. Check with the hotel or place you may be staying to see if a service charge has already been added to the bill. This is the practice in many foreign countries and takes care of the matter very efficiently.

Many guidebooks list pages of suggested amounts to tip for various services. Because your holiday is not intended to be spent computing percentages, I suggest you simply ask when in doubt and pay in accordance to the type of service rendered. Remember, you should not feel intimidated because you do not know the custom. Asking will give you the answers.

Here are a few simple guidelines. Learn which coin is worth about a quarter in terms of each country's standard of living and keep many in a separate purse. Start each day with this reserve handy for the porters, waiters and washroom attendants. Some persons do rely on tipping as their sole source of income, although the rules will vary from country to country.

The sidewalk cafes are a delightful custom in many parts of the world. You can sit for hours and when you do, leave a tip to compensate the waiter for the long time you kept the table. Many of these informal eating places will include in large letters on the bill, Service Not Included. Many places, and especially eating establishments, do include a percentage for service and it is important to know this or you will be tipping on top of tip.

Transportation

The variance of price structures in the field of transportation is complex and forever changing. The agent is a specialist to whom you can turn over the enormous time consuming chore of dovetailing schedules, confirming hotel, rail, and car rentals. You will be handed a complete packet. Keep the vouchers safe. They represent the individual confirmations for hotels, car, and sightseeing trips and are your proof of payment. Even the detailed typed itineraries, with extra copies for friends and relatives, are supplied by the travel agent.

Remember the trip diary described in an earlier chapter. Jot information the agent gives you directly on pages within the diary. This is a piece of information I received a long time ago from one of my favorite travel agents. Take along large manila envelopes that you have addressed to your home address. Slip these along the side or on the bottom of your case. They take a small amount of space; however, the space they will save you is considerable. Here is how they are used:

You will find the guidebooks, postal card souvenirs, and other papers have a habit of multiplying as you move along in your travels. Because you may want to keep them for future reference, slip them into the manila envelope and use the special rate allowed for book and printed matter to send the items.

A word of caution when you prepare anything to send is be selective. Remember the motto: "Less is more."

Hotels

A word about advance hotel booking abroad. There will be many who simply state: "Don't bother, there is always a room and it allows great flexibility if one does not have reservations.''

For this type of thinking, you may benefit from the personal testimony of an experienced, retired teacher who had traveled abroad every year for several months each summer. She had formerly been of the school—''never make a reservation.'' That year she decided to travel in early spring. It happened to be during Easter and she arrived in Rome without reservations. As was her practice, she went directly to the city's tourist office to ask their help in finding accommodations. Each place could provide only a single night and she spent each day hunting for another bed. She admits there was not a person to blame except herself; however, over and over there are thousands of travelers who suffer the same disappointments. Do take the precaution of arranging confirmed accommodations for the first few days. It proves far too expensive to lose your time and exhaust yourself in the frustration of seeking lodging.

My personal observation about the large, deluxe hotels abroad is that the elegance and perfection of the expensive and world renowned hotels is sought by those wishing privacy, prestige of name and address, and the attention and service that is equated with the price and reputation. With the elegance and the privacy comes little warmth and conversation. Meeting people is important to the woman alone and if you are arranging the reservations, or have instructed your travel agent about your preference, keep in mind the benefits of first-class hotels or deluxe pensions. During my years of travel, I have found first class does mean the best the place has to offer. It may not guarantee a private bath; but, it will be comfortable and not as costly as deluxe accommodations. American tastes can usually find comfort with the first- and second-class hotels. But any hotel rated as third or fourth class is very unlikely to add much pleasure to your trip. Be guided by your travel agent or any of the excellent Guide Michelin books on the market. Should you be traveling in

Spain or Portugal, you may consider the hotels supervised by the government. They are known as albergues and paradores in Spain. In Portugal, look for the pousadas and if you are traveling the countryside, they will prove inexpensive and clean rooms for you.

Pensions

For the traveler seeking a vacation with a foreign flair, I encourage staying in several pensions along the way. You will enjoy the warmth of a small, family atmosphere; and, as the word does mean boardinghouse in French, it is exactly as it states. Because the pension may vary greatly, it is important to select cautiously. Ask your travel agent for first-hand information about the pensions in the countries you plan to visit. The owner often requires you to take three meals a day; but, you may pay the full board and enjoy the bed and perhaps only the morning meal, or an occasional evening meal with the family. The price of the entire package is still well under any rate of a commercial hotel that would not include any meals in their room price. The meals are prearranged courses and served at a fixed hour in the pension you have chosen. The menu will reflect the term, "table d'hote" and it literally is translated to mean "the host's table." Another result of the arrangement is definitely to your advantage; it calms you down to a pace that is essential if you are going to relax on a vacation and be good to yourself. Meet the natives, live with the people, see life as others do and your horizons will open. When you are a guest in the pension, Monsieur and Madame les Patrons can be helpful to you in a dozen different ways.

As with everything, it is important to be alert to the minus side of pension lodging. Because of the inexpensive rates, you may be in the company of the very young student crowd and the older couples with limited incomes. As I mentioned earlier, do not take the time of a holiday to start a strict budget program. The price should not be the determining factor in your decision to try a week at a pension. The question goes back to your own personal desires and what you expect on your vacation. If you are attracted to the big city life and want the excitement of the metropolitan beat—a pension will be dim by comparison.

Paying Guest Home

When you see the initials P.G. they refer to an arrangement of living with a foreign family, and I encourage you to seek more information if you think it might be for you. Ask the national tourist office in the country you are visiting. The Paris Welcome Information Office is The Accueil de France. A list of host families will be provided and you may make arrangements according to your needs. In London there are a large number of very good Paying Guest agencies and I am personally most familiar with the official Non-commercial Accommodation Service, 64 St. James Street, London S.E. 1. They will send you information on the apartments that are available to rent by the week and longer. I am very partial to London and the surrounding country because of an early experience during my employment with ARAMCO (Arabian American Oil Company), when I was based in New York and flying trips to the Middle East. It was possible to arrange several weeks between flights, and for the price of one-week lodging at a deluxe London hotel, I was able to rent a flat for two months. The key to thoroughly enjoying any city, country, or place, is always the people you meet and the warmth of feeling you belong. You may wish to trade a planned week at another spot for a week's stay where you are. Even though you may have been booked at an expensive first-class, centrally located hotel, another week's rest and pleasure as a paying guest with a family, or in a pension or a hostel may be an experience that proves to be the highlight of your trip.

Eurailpass

You can get almost anywhere in Europe by train and if you plan to cover a lot of territory, consider the Eurail and the Britrail Pass. One *must* purchase these passes before leaving the United States. Ask your travel agent and he will arrange to get them for you, or will provide you with the instructions and the address. For current information regarding European trains, the Eurail Guide by Saltzman and Muileman will provide details on rail itineraries, fares, and schedules. A Eurailpass entitles you to unlimited first-class travel on trains in thirteen or more European countries. Time periods extend from two weeks to three months and the passes range from $170 to $420. Speaking from personal experience when traveling one summer with our family, the use of a Swissrail Pass proved a bargain and a convenience. The five of us could zip all over Switzerland, using Zurich as our base of operation. We would spend a day in Lucerne and take the train back to Zurich in time for late dinner and rest. Back on the train the next day for a two-day stay in Berne and return again to Zurich. When the rains fell steadily in Zurich, a suggestion to travel south to Lugano resulted in a week of sunshine and pleasure in exploring the south of Switzerland. Our return north was purposely booked on the comfortable TEE* train. For a small additional charge, one may reserve a couchette compartment and the train traveling during night hours thus serves as a hotel on wheels.

Take note of an important fact regarding European trains. Always make sure the particular car you are on is bound for your destination because you may board the right train that happens not to end up in the right town. The European trains have a disconcerting habit of shedding cars. Another helpful bit of advice is to brown bag your train travels. Pick up some of the delicious cheeses, sausage, and a loaf of crusty

---

*Trans Europ Express—highspeed European train.

bread. Ask about the wines and explain you want an especially nice bottle to take on your "picnic." The merchant will be flattered you asked and be assured that his recommendation will be exceptional.

Excellent Sources of Reference

The volumes of travel books available today cover every possible aspect of travel. Many list places to stay, where to eat, what to do, and the "be sure to see" list.

I favor the personal touch of a hand-by-hand guide. One such man is George W. Oakes and his popular *Turn Right at the Fountain* series. The first series appeared in the New York Times in 1961 with this endorsement: "By following George W. Oakes' walks, you will get a good over-all impression of what is considered most worthwhile and unusual in each city." Mr. Oakes believes the only way to get to know a city is by walking through it. This provides the chance to explore the hidden byways and the unusual places which do give every city its own character. What better way to understand the city and to feel the way of life?

Visit your favorite bookstore and many excellent writings will help you in planning and preparing for the trip. Inquire about the European edition of *Country Inns and Back Roads,* Berkshire Traveller Press in Stockbridge, Mass. 01262. A favorite of many over the past ten years is the North America publication of *Country Inns and Back Roads* and I found the European guide equally as good. Pick up a word and phrase book such as Fielding's *American Traveler's Companion.*

Turn to the resource list at the back of this book for additional references and keep alert to the recommendations of the travel section of your newspaper and, always, the library.

Sinking into the Culture

This is a phrase used by another of my travel agent friends and it appropriately tells the tourist how to become a traveler. Think of yourself as a resident and it will do wonders for the attitude you have toward the country and its people. Plan time to leisurely explore and to sink into the culture of the place you are visiting. Your vacation time should be captured moments of pure luxury. Never plan a pace that will have you feeling rushed and running. Demand the control of your hours and treat them in exactly the way you enjoy most.

A well-known travel editor is often quoted expressing her pet phrase: "Never allow time to pinch because you attempt too much." If you plan a theater for the evening, tour in the morning and plan a relaxed and simple afternoon in the full anticipation of an evening you will remember for always.

Consider a weekend boat trip and you will have an excellent opportunity to meet people, enjoy the change of pace and spend time on the water. The ferry from Copenhagen to Malmo, Sweden, or the ferry from Istanbul across the Bosporus to Asia are examples. A shorter day trip is a "must" when in Paris and the thrill of boarding the bateaux mouche that tour the Seine from the Pont d'Iena in Paris. Take the canal boats in Amsterdam and enjoy a leisurely trip through the city.

Terms You'll Be Glad You Know

Do not assume the "C" on tub and washbowl taps means cold in the South American countries, or Spain, France, or Italy. Calda (Italian), Chaude (French), Caliente (Spanish) all mean scalding. Do keep this in mind when seeing the "C."

Cold water will be marked "F" for friggia (Italian), froide (French), frio (Spanish). Germany and Austria show "K" for kalt meaning cold.

To make a telephone call from a pay station on the Continent, you will need a token or a slug. They are called in

France, a jeton; in Italy, gettone; and in Spain, the ficha. The instructions for using the phone may be confusing and it is best to ask for help. For instance, in many countries, you will lose your token if you put it in before you dial the number.

Language

It is helpful if you speak the language of the country you are visiting; however, with a simple phrase book you can memorize a basic vocabulary. Consider a minimum of these words: please, thank you, excuse me, you are welcome, good morning, good evening, goodbye, how much, where, yes, no, and do you speak English? This will provide much help and you will find many people speak English and are pleased you have attempted to speak a few words of their language.

Carry the phrase book with you for the times you will need to look up specific words. You may find use for the book several times each day.

This may sound basic; however, before you leave a hotel in a foreign country in a taxi, walking, or public transportation, take the name and address of the hotel with you. Nothing could be more important when you have become lost in a strange place, do not speak the language and have a lapse of memory as to where you are indeed staying, than to have taken a piece of the hotel stationery or packet of matches with the name and address of the hotel which you can show to the taxi driver or to anyone who can help you.

Terms You Should Know

MAP—Modified American Plan. The hotel rate includes a substantial breakfast and dinner. You are responsible for your own luncheon.

EP—European Plan means accommodations only. This is

preferred when you enjoy exploring new restaurants and places to dine other than the hotel.

AP—American Plan includes hotel rate and three meals. Oftentimes a self-contained resort offers this plan because everything is a long distance from the hotel.

Concierge—An ally on the European Continent is this gentleman in a blue uniform with gold braid and a crossed-keys insignia on the lapels. Perhaps the most important staff member you will meet in any hotel, he performs a multitude of services that American hotel desk clerk, travel desk, bell captain, doorman, social hostess, and manager all do. The simplicity of asking one man to do any and all of these services does result in convenience. Tip him generously and ask him for all the above help. Provide the tip in an envelope clearly marked "Concierge" when you check out.

Consulate—Your friend in need. Provides a special welfare and protective agency for all American tourists. If you are in trouble, you will receive emergency assistance. If injured or seriously ill, the best medical care is suggested. If you lose your money and must reach your family back home, the consulate will act as an intermediary. Any passport that expires, is lost or stolen may be issued, renewed, amended, or even extended. In brief, anytime your life and liberty may be threatened, the comfort of knowing the American Consulate is a friend does serve to bridge the gap of those traveling abroad.

Custom of Queuing-up—This is the considerate custom of awaiting one's turn and is recognized everywhere in England. Waiting for buses, taxis, and in post offices, banks, stores and wherever transportation and service is provided. To "queue-up" is to take one's place behind the person who is waiting in line.

Centigrade—To convert a foreign thermometer reading from Centigrade to Fahrenheit: Double any Centigrade figure above zero, subtract ten percent, and add thirty-two. This gives you the equivalent temperature in Fahrenheit.

Bidet—Pronounced bee-day. A ceramic basin shaped like a saddle and found in most European bathrooms. Its purpose is personal hygiene for both men and women. First invented in France, it has been used for centuries throughout Europe, South America and wherever the pattern of living is European.

Kilogram—A kilogram equals about two and two-tenths pounds. Convert kilos to pounds by doubling the figure. Add ten percent to the doubled figure.

Kilometer—A kilometer is about five-eighths of a mile or in round numbers sixty percent. Convert kilometers to miles by multiplying by six and moving the decimal point one digit to the left.

IAMAT–International Association for Medical Assistance to Travelers is the definition of IAMAT. Founded many years ago by Dr. Marcolongo, it is a nonprofit organization with medical centers established in nearly seventy countries on all continents and with English speaking physicians on twenty-four hour call. The offices are in New York, Switzerland and in Canada. Write for additional information to:

IAMAT
Empire State Building
350 Fifth Ave., Suite 5620
New York, New York 10001

If you request membership in IAMAT, you will not be charged. However, you are asked to give any donation you can afford for the privilege of belonging. Upon receipt of your membership card, you will receive a directory of doctors and, also, two important brochures. They are the Traveler Clinical Record and the World Immunization and Malaria Risk Chart. Fill the Traveler Clinical Record out with your doctor's assistance and carry this in your passport case. The card provides information important to a doctor treating you overseas. Information such as any medication you are taking, sensitivities to drugs, allergies, blood type and an immunization record. Additionally, a summary of cardiac condition, your diabetic condition and anticoagulant drugs taken for any heart condition.

The second brochure, the Malaria Risk Chart, is self-explanatory. The two brochures and the record card are emergency items that every traveler should carry.

All of us would hope for a carefree holiday and never to be reminded of illness or emergency. However, to remove the anxiety by being prepared is the ounce of prevention that we have been taught is worth the pound of cure.

Shopping Abroad

Shopping can be a pleasant bonus to every trip to foreign countries. Perhaps it is true that almost everything which can be purchased abroad is available at home; but, the joy of discovery is exciting and fun. When you see exactly what you want in some small shop off the beaten track, my advice is to buy it immediately. Chances of your returning to the same shop, or even being able to find the street, are not in your favor. An impulse purchase may prove a delight for years to come.

Over the years I have collected some experience and advice I will share. I seriously recommend saying no nicely to requests you may have from well-meaning neighbors or relatives who ask you to shop for them. Such a commitment can turn shopping into an obligation and spoil the fun and freedom of your trip. Select a well-known store, shop for those on your list and mail your selections direct to the recipient.

Duty-Free and What It Means—Another great saving of both time and money while traveling is the duty-free port which provides a large selection of merchandise in one place at bargain prices. The credit for and explanation of "Duty-Free" must go to the Irish. In 1947, the Irish Parliament ruled that any goods brought directly into the Shannon Airport from abroad would not be liable to duty or local taxes. That decision started the phenomenal growth of duty-free shopping throughout the world. The goods sold in duty-free shops are lower than their equivalent in the United States because every government levies duties on certain imported goods to protect its industries. The government can lift those duties when it chooses and the savings is considerable when a consumer purchases duty-free merchandise. Strict control is exercised and only those in transit may buy duty-free items. The amount you may purchase is unlimited and payment may be made with major credit cards, currency from any country you have visited, traveler's checks and U.S. cash.

Ships and Cruises—Many Caribbean cruises schedule several ports of call for the benefit of enthusiastic shoppers. Duty-free shopping is a beloved institution in most of the Caribbean, Canary and Virgin Islands. Purchases are delivered directly to the ship and the convenience encourages buying.

Customs—Customs laws and regulations will differ from country to country. Check with your airline or travel agent before you go. The written declaration that you will be required to fill out before going through customs is simple when you have kept all of your sales slips in one place. It is also an excellent plan to pack everything you have purchased in a separate bag and have this case and your sales slips to verify the items you listed on the declaration form. As a resident of the U.S. you may acquire goods valued up to $100.00 total retail value without payment of duty providing you have been outside of the United States for at least forty-eight hours. Any balance over the $100.00 will be subject to customs duties.

You have the privilege of mailing gifts with value under

$10.00 home without duty payment. The number of individual $10.00 gifts may be as many as you like; however, not more than one parcel a day should be received by the same person to qualify for the duty-free exemption. Mark the package "gift under $10.00." Some things you are not allowed to send are alcohol, tobacco or perfumes. Also, you will not be allowed to bring back into the U.S. any fresh fruit, meat, or meat products, vegetables, plants or seeds.

A copy of the booklet "Know Before You Go" or "U.S. Customs Hints for Returning Residents" may be picked up from a local Customs or passport office, or you may send for it by writing to:

Superintendent of Documents
U.S. Government Printing Office
Washington, D.C. 20402

The booklet contains rates of duty on frequently purchased items and gives a full explanation on restrictions and limitations.

No Duty—Antiques over one hundred years old can be brought in free of duty. Also, unframed, original, signed art when accompanied by the artist's receipt and genuine pearls are allowed free of duty. Ask about other items.

Bargains—Where?—Powdered saffron in little packets from Spain. This is an expensive spice in the U.S. It is a thoughtful gift for your friends who enjoy cooking. French perfume purchased at a duty-free shop is oftentimes about half the price you pay in the U.S. English bone china and Irish Waterford crystal are lovely buys. Cashmere is an exceptional buy in London and the selection of all styles and sizes at the Shannon airport allows a last minute purchase of this luxury item at a fantastic savings over the prices one pays in the United States.

I have just returned from Florence and can honestly report the best prices for the finest workmanship. The leather goods are excellent and reasonable. I found gold jewelry less expensive than in the West Indies (Curacao has a reputation for great prices); however, Florence was even better and the selection unlimited. The solid silver pieces are better priced than Mexico and engraving beautifully finished with only a few hours notice. I recommend the shops along the Ponte Vecchio (the old bridge that survived even the German bombs during the World War and whose history has held traditionally to keeping the jewelry shops along the bridge). Cameos are a specialty and are made into lovely rings, bracelets and necklaces. The many excellent galleries are plentiful in Florence and have some of the very best prints and reproductions.

If you visit Switzerland, the savings on watches will be about forty percent depending on your choice. A word about the famous Swiss chocolate. Buy it in the U.S. because any attempt at carrying this item will mean extra bulk, a nuisance when it melts, and the delicious liqueur filled chocolate will not be allowed through customs.

Germany is known for the precision goods such as cameras, binoculars, eyeglasses and telescopes. The savings is about twenty to twenty-five percent and you can be assured of top quality in all goods.

The Orient can best be described as one large shop when spending time in Hong Kong and Tokyo. Arrange for a guide to help you understand the best buys and where to find them. If pressed for time, the hotel arcade shops are filled with lovely items that are delightful memories of your holiday. The joy of remembering the place and the moment of purchase is often as enjoyable as the gift itself. Shop wisely but don't deny yourself the beauty of surroundings and the comfort and convenience that hotel and specialty shops provide. Of course, you are paying a certain amount for the atmosphere, the location and the service, and why shouldn't you? This is your holiday and your time to enjoy and do just that.

For direct contrast to the above-mentioned luxury try:

Flea Markets—You haven't really shopped until you experience the digging and haggling that is part of searching for hidden treasures in a flea market. As you walk smugly away from the scene with your discovery wrapped adequately in an old newspaper, you will experience a feeling of triumph. The atmosphere is both depressing and fascinating; and, if you have the stamina and the ability to recognize the real from the fake, I encourage you and only wish that I could join you. The chance of finding something marvelous among the tangle of odds and ends lends an aura of magic to the markets.

Here are a few basics to keep in mind that will guide you toward a great experience and alert you to a few things you should avoid.

1. Dress for the occasion. Wear comfortable shoes and your oldest clothes. Be aware that all markets are the favorite haunts of pickpockets. Avoid taking handbags. It is best to carry money in your pockets when possible. A string or large cloth shopping bag will help carry your purchases.

2. Before you fall victim to an oversized piece of anything, consider the cost of shipment and duty, which, when added to the purchase price may dim your enthusiasm.

3. Markets are not usually open every day. Many have hours in the early morning and close by noon. Sunday is the popular day that you will find the majority of them doing business. Check with the hotel porter and plan your days accordingly with plans to give up sleep the morning you go. Competition for choice items is keen and the earlier you start, the better your chances.

4. Haggling has been part of the markets (also referred to as bazaars) in North Africa, the Middle East and Asia for years. When shopping in these countries, the original price quoted is merely an acknowledged starting point and bar-

gaining is an essential part of the negotiations. To the novice, an instant lesson in learning how is absorbed by simply listening. You will find it's easy and the merchant enjoys the haggling about price even more than you. Don't miss this opportunity if you are visiting any country where this is accepted practice. My memories of purchases during the years I worked in the Middle East for ARAMCO are vivid today as I recall the excitement of bargaining in Lebanon, Beirut, Daharan, and Jedda in Saudi Arabia. On one special occasion, driving to Damascus, we stopped an Arab with a sack of jewelry slung across his back. A purchase does take on memories for a lifetime when made in the middle of the desert and it is this type of buying that I want you to experience.

5. Finally, a word of caution about buying at a market or bazaar. The man who runs the stall has no obligation to sell an authentic product. The motto is: "Let the buyer beware." My advice is to buy what pleases your eye and if you happen to select something of value it will provide an even added bonus later. Let the priority of having an interesting experience and one you will long remember be your reason for shopping and I guarantee you a great day.

It has been said a book is really not complete until it has a reader. Also true, is the fact a play has not concluded without the applause. I like to equate the return home from a trip with a feeling of personal applause.

In the words of Edward Gibbon, "I was never less alone than when by myself." And you too, will realize the best type of company to enjoy is with that person you know best. That person is "you."

RESOURCES

AIR TRAVEL: Jim Woodman's Air Travel Bargains Guide is revised annually and distributed by Simon & Schuster, Inc., New York. An encyclopedia of fares, airlines and aircraft, bargain air tours. Ask your travel agent or check with your local book store.

AMERICAN RIVER TOURING ASSOCIATION: ARTA was founded in 1963 as a non-profit organization dedicated to teaching the basic skills necessary to enjoy our wilderness, waterways, rivers, lakes, and seacoasts. For information: River Adventure ARTA, 1016 Jackson Street, Oakland, California, 94607

AMERICAN SOCIETY OF TRAVEL AGENTS: ASTA, 360 Lexington Avenue, New York, New York, 10017. Ask for the name and address of travel agents in your area. Membership assures you the agent has met certain criteria in order to qualify for membership in the American Society of Travel Agents.

AMERICAN TELEPHONE AND TELEGRAPH COMPANY LONG LINES DEPARTMENT: Mr. L. R. Clark, Room 843, Five World Trade Center, New York, New York, 10048. This free service for Americans traveling abroad offers three pocket reference guides devoted to *Getting Around Overseas.* Includes information on time differences, weights and measures chart, foreign word translations and currency conversion tables. Also, a comprehensive list of U.S. Embassies and Consulates and telephone rates from the U.S. to many foreign countries.

AUTOMOBILE TRAVEL: American Automobile Association offers a brochure outlining the services provided. Write to: AAA, 8111 Gatehouse Road, Falls Church, Virginia, 22042. Also, ask for the address of office nearest you.

BUS TRAVEL: Continental Trailways Tours, 181 O'Farrell Street, San Francisco, California, 94102. Greyhound, Inc., Greyhound Tower, Phoenix, Arizona, 85077

CRUISES: Ford's International Cruise Guide and Ford's Freighter Travel Guide are both comprehensive sources of sea travel information. Available at bookstores, they are both published twice a year. May be ordered direct: International Cruise Guide or Freighter Travel Guide, 22030 Ventura Blvd., Suite B, Woodland Hills, California, 91365. Princess Cruises, 2020 Avenue of the Stars, Los Angeles, California, 90067. Prudential Lines, One California Street, San Francisco, California, 94106. Royal Caribbean, 903 South American Way, Miami, Florida, 33132. Royal Viking Lines, 1 Embarcadero Center, San Francisco, California, 94111. Sitmar Cruises, 10100 Santa Monica Blvd., Los Angeles, California, 90067.

TRAIN TRAVEL: Amtrak Travel Center, P.O. Box 20987, Los Angeles, California, 90006, or, P.O. Box 3000, Bellmore, New York, 11710, or, P.O. Box 4733, Chicago, Illinois, 60680.

EURAILPASS or STUDENT RAILPASS: Write to Eurailpass, P.O. Box 90, Bohemia, New York, 11716.

Note: Eurailpasses, Swiss Rail and Britrail passes must be purchased before you leave the United States. You may purchase them from your travel agent or respective tourist office.

Ireland Rambler Ticket is the train pass used in The Republic of Ireland. Check with an office of Irish Tourist Board for information and fare schedules.

TRAVEL WITH CHILDREN, BOOKS AND SUGGESTIONS: Kiester, Edwin Jr. *How and Where To Vacation With Children and Enjoy It.* New York: Doubleday & Company, 1964. Hadley, Leila *How To Travel With Children In Europe.* New York: Walker and Company, 1964.

Great suggestions when visiting New York with children.

NEW YORK EXPERIENCE: Complete show every hour daily. And from the comfort of an armchair, one travels visually through all that is New York City. Fabulous extravaganza of sight, sound, and sensations. Located in McGraw-Hill Bldg. The lower Plaza at 6th Avenue between 48th and 49th Street. PH: 212/869-0345.

UNITED NATIONS HEADQUARTERS: Located on 18 acre site between First Avenue and East River from 42nd to 48th Streets. One hour guided tours from 9–4:45 p.m.

EMPIRE OBSERVATORY: Fifth Avenue and 34th Street. Open 9:30 till midnight every day.

STUDENT TRAVEL: Council on International Education Exchange, 777 United Nations Plaza, New York, New York, 10017. Council on International Education Exchange, 235 East Santa Clara Street, Suite 710, San Jose, California, 95113.

TRAVELING WITH PETS: *Touring with Towser* is a handy guide to traveling with pets. The Gaines Dog Research Center directory lists thousands of hotels and motels in the United States and in Canada that will welcome your pets. To obtain a copy, send 50¢ to: Gaines TWT, P.O. Box 1007, Kankakee, Illinois, 60901.

SPECIAL SERVICES: *Travel for the Handicapped* is a unique service conducted by Evergreen Travel Service. For information write to them: 19492 44th Avenue West, Lynnwood, Washington. *The Wheelchair Traveler:* P.O. Box 169, Woodlands Hills, California, 91364. *Tours for the Deaf* Ide H. Schmidt c/o Embassy Travel, 247 South Country Place, Palm Beach, Florida.

HEALTH: *How To Travel the World and Stay Healthy* ARCO, $1.45, your bookstore. *Medical Advice for the Traveler* Popular Library. *Medic Alert Foundation* P.O. Box 1009, Turlock, California, 95380. International Association for Medical Assistance, Empire State Building, 350 Fifth Avenue, #5620, New York, New York, 10001. *Health Spas World Guide Book to Health Spas, Mineral Baths and Nature Cure Centers.* Yaller, Robert and Rave. Santa Barbara, California, Woodridge Press Publishing Company.

EARPLUGS: Write J. D. Brown, 2 Embarcadero Center, San Francisco, California, 94111

EUROPEAN INFORMATION FOR TRAVEL: *Electrical Appliances Abroad:* A free booklet will solve the mystery of electricity in foreign travel. Send a self-addressed, business sized envelope to:

> Foreign Electricity is No Deep Secret
> Franzus Company
> 352 Park Avenue South
> New York, New York 10010

American Traveler's Companion by Gradon S. DeLand. Fielding's conversation guide to Europe Word and Phrase book. Available in paperback at bookstores.

Travelers Instant Money Converter: by Edward Rondthaler. New York: Grosset & Dunlap, Inc. Available at bookstores.

Instant Metric Converter published by New York: Doubleday and Company. Available at bookstores.

PASSPORT: For information about passport application and renewal, contact your local office. If you do not have one in your city, full information under one cover may be sent to you. Write: Passport Office, U.S. Department of State, 1245 K Street, Northwest, Washington, D.C., 20524.

MENU TRANSLATERS: Excellent menu translaters for Europe are the Marling Menu Masters. They are slim and hold a wealth of information. Write to: Menu Master, Rough and Ready, California.

SINGLEWORLD: Cruises and Tours for single people of all ages. Gramercy's Singleworld, formerly Bachelor Party Tours, 444 Madison Avenue, New York, New York, 10022.

CLUB MED INC.: For information see your travel agent or write: Club Med Inc., 40 West 57th Street, New York, New York, 10019.

Space does not permit this limited resource list to cover all that is available today. Hopefully, this information will help to guide you and result in additional research and reading. Libraries are an excellent source and should be used generously when planning a trip. The travel sections of your local bookstores and the Sunday travel issues in newspapers can prove an incentive and helpful to anyone wishing to vacation. Ask your travel agent for his advice on reading materials, brochures and guides to help in preparing you for the trip. Allow yourself comfortable time to enjoy reading about your planned destinations and the result is a glorious and rewarding adventure in travel.

BIBLIOGRAPHY

American Airlines Booklet "The American Woman's Way."

American Airlines Booklet "The Traveling Woman."

Adams, Eleanor. *How to Plan Your Vacation and Enjoy It.* New York: Nelson Doubleday, Inc.

Adams, Eleanor. *Your Trip To Europe.* New York: Nelson Doubleday, Inc., 1966.

Baer, Jean. *Follow Me!* New York: The Macmillan Company, 1965.

Bracken, Peg. *But I Wouldn't Have Missed It For The World,* Fawcett Publications, Greenwich, Conn. 1974.

Carnegie, Dale. *Public Speaking and Influencing Men In Business.* American Book-Stratford Press, Inc. New York.

Cole, Luella and Lowie, Robert H. *A Practical Handbook for Planning a Trip to Europe.* New York: Vantage Press, Inc. 1957.

Garth, Sheridan H. and Kaufman, William I. *Cook's Pocket Travel Guide to Europe.* New York, Pocket Books, Inc. 1963.

Girson, Rochelle. *Maiden Voyages*. A Lively guide for the Woman Traveler. New York: Harcourt, Brace & World, Inc. 1967.

Glamour Magazine. "How To Plan A Trip," February, 1976.

Glamour Magazine. "Where To Go What To Do Around the World," May, 1976.

Gonzalez, Arturo F. Jr. *How To Find Travel Bargains After Reaching Europe,* National Observer week ending April 9, 1977.

Harper's Bazaar. "News from Club Mediterranee," August 1976.

Harris, Janet. *The Prime of Ms. America. The American Woman at 40*. Signet, 1975.

Hesse, Georgia. *Going My Way,* San Francisco: Chronicle Books, 1975.

Hilliard, Marion Dr. *Women and Fatigue*. New York: Doubleday & Company, Inc. 1960.

Kenis, Adrea. *The Single Girl's Guide to Europe*. New York: Paperback Library, 1969.

Koltun, Frances. *The Intelligent Woman Traveler*. New York: Simon and Schuster, 1967.

Meyer, Edith Patterson. *Go It Alone, Lady!* The Woman's Guide to European Travel. New York: Harper and Brothers Publishers, 1957.

New York Times, "For The Woman On Her Own: Trust People Within Limits." by Virginia Miles, October 31, 1976.

Og, Mandino. *A Treasury of Success Unlimited*. New York: Hawthorn Books, 1973.

Olson, Harvey S. *Olson's Complete Travel Guide to Europe Aboard and Abroad*. New York: J. B. Lippincott, 1956.

Roulston, Marjorie Hillis. *Keep Going and Like It*. New York: Doubleday and Company, Inc., 1967.

Rule, Colter, M.D. *A Traveler's Guide to Good Health,* New York: Doubleday and Company, 1960.

Syvertsen, Edythe. *Travel Tips.* New York: Grosset & Dunlap, Tempo Books, 1976.

Tully, Gerie. *Especially for Women.* New York: Abelard-Schuman, 1975.

Van Campens, Shirley. *Travel and the Single Woman.* Sacramento: Prule Publishing Corporation, 1976.

Vogue Magazine. Travel editor's article on packing, December 1976.

Woman's Day. "Looking for a New Lease on Life? Try a Cruise." October 1976.

Woman's Day, "January Getaways," January, 1977.

Yates, Martha. *Coping.* New York: Prentice Hall, Inc. 1976.

QUICK REFERENCE GUIDE

THE EVERYWOMAN'S GUIDE SERIES

EVERYWOMAN'S GUIDE TO COLLEGE
Eileen Gray
176 pages, $3.95

A logical, no-nonsense study of the emotional, financial and academic realities
of the returning woman student of any age. It includes sections on how to finance
yourself in school and a field-by-field employment outlook for the woman
college graduate through 1980.

EVERYWOMAN'S GUIDE TO FINANCIAL INDEPENDENCE
Mavis Arthur Groza
144 pages, $3.95

Rich or poor, single or married, every woman's questions about how to handle
finances are answered in this comprehensive money book. It covers investing,
budgeting, credit, insurance, estate planning, saving and security, as well as the
new credit laws and government programs affecting the monetary concerns of
women.

EVERYWOMAN'S GUIDE TO A NEW IMAGE
Peggy Granger
128 pages, $3.95

This practical guide presents a range of new ideas — from bioenergetic analysis
to I Ching to humanistic psychology — along with a series of interviews with
women who have successfully translated these theories into practical and
meaningful changes in their lives.

EVERYWOMAN'S GUIDE TO POLITICAL AWARENESS
Phyllis Butler and Dorothy Gray
128 pages, $3.95

This is a fact-filled handbook for all women who want a positive introduction
to institutional and power politics. It reviews the political structure, types
of activity (volunteer, political, pro, candidate), how to get involved, basic
do's and don'ts, the running of a campaign, and much much more.

EVERYWOMAN'S GUIDE TO TIME MANAGEMENT
Donna Goldfein
128 pages, $3.95

A back-to-basics, step-by-step program tailored to help homemaker or professional who is bogged down by routine to take charge of her life by establishing priorities, setting time limits, scheduling realistically, communicating effectively, sim-
plifying tasks, and anticipating problems.

Available at your local book or department store or directly from the publisher.
To order by mail, send check or money order to:

Les Femmes Publishing
231 Adrian Road
Suite MPB
Millbrae, California 94030

Please include 50 cents for postage and handling. California residents add 6% tax.